The Creative Arts in Governance of Urban Renewal and Development

This book focuses on the role of the creative sector in the governance of urban renewal and economic development initiatives.

Rory Shand examines the ways in which both the top-down nature of the creative sector, and the bottom-up roles of creative arts organisations, drive development and engage with local communities or areas in regeneration projects that target employment, training and education, as well as social engagement. Underpinning these projects are governance mechanisms, through delivery, funding and participation. Drawing on case studies from the UK, Germany and Canada, Shand compares national creative sector policies and creative arts bodies engaged in the governance of urban renewal and development programmes, as well as including a comparative chapter offering an overview of best and worst practice, which also examines and summarises the key themes across both theory and practice. In his concluding remarks, he highlights and discusses the key challenges posed by governance mechanisms to urban renewal and economic development programmes and identifies future comparative case studies in the field.

This book will be of great interest to students of environmental studies, public policy and politics and geography, as well as being a relevant resource for practitioners from NGOs, local and national levels of governments and community projects.

Rory Shand is Reader in Political Economy, Manchester Metropolitan University, UK.

Routledge Explorations in Environmental Studies

Poetics of the Earth
Natural History and Human History
Augustin Berque

Environmental Humanities and the Uncanny
Ecoculture, Literature and Religion
Rod Giblett

Ethical Responses to Nature's Call
Reticent Imperatives
James Magrini

Environmental Education in Indonesia
Creating Responsible Citizens in the Global South?
Lyn Parker and Kelsie Prabawa-Sear

Ecofeminism and the Indian Novel
Sangita Patil

The Role of Non-state Actors in the Green Transition
Building a Sustainable Future
Edited by Jens Hoff, Quentin Gausset and Simon Lex

The Creative Arts in Governance of Urban Renewal and Development
Rory Shand

What Can *I* do to Heal the World?
Haydn Washington

Towards a Society of Degrowth
Onofrio Romano

www.routledge.com/Routledge-Explorations-in-Environmental-Studies/book-series/REES

The Creative Arts in Governance of Urban Renewal and Development

Rory Shand

Routledge
Taylor & Francis Group
LONDON AND NEW YORK

earthscan
from Routledge

First published 2020 by Routledge

2 Park Square, Milton Park, Abingdon, Oxon OX14 4RN
605 Third Avenue, New York, NY 10017

Routledge is an imprint of the Taylor & Francis Group, an informa business

First issued in paperback 2022

Publisher's Note

The publisher has gone to great lengths to ensure the quality of this reprint but points out that some imperfections in the original copies may be apparent.

British Library Cataloguing-in-Publication Data
A catalogue record for this book is available from the British Library

Library of Congress Cataloging-in-Publication Data
A catalog record has been requested for this book

ISBN: 978-1-138-67513-1 (hbk)
ISBN: 978-1-03-233598-8 (pbk)
DOI: 10.4324/9781315560823

Typeset in Sabon
by Wearset Ltd, Boldon, Tyne and Wear

Contents

Tables

Boxes

Acknowledgements

First, I wish to thank my editor on this book, Matt Shobbrook, and the other members of the editorial team at Routledge engaged in the project. I also want to extend special mention and thanks to Professor Duncan Cameron, Dr Sam Garwood and Jacob Nickles (University of Sheffield), both as colleagues and as friends. My colleagues and friends at Manchester Metropolitan University have been a wonderful source of ideas and support throughout the project – as they are in all things – and I extend my sincere thanks to all of them but especially to Professor Donna Lee, Dr Craig Berry, Professor Jon Grix, Dr Kathryn Simpson, Dr David Beel, Dr Richard Whittle, Christian Spence, Dr Nick O'Donovan, Dr Adam Barber and Professor Carol Atkinson. As always, friends have contributed to this work through their humour and support, and I thank them all, but especially Steve, Graham and Al. My family as ever have been a wonderful support and inspiration, and I thank them, especially Margaret and John Shand, LL, Mila and Furby, and Helen, to whom this book is dedicated.

Rory Shand
Manchester

1 The creative arts in governance of urban renewal and development

When we imagine the creative arts, what do we picture? Do we see an image of a whispered discussion beside a famous portrait in a grand gallery, perhaps; a music festival, or orchestra; a photograph or film of a natural phenomenon; or maybe a sculpture? Do we equate these ideas with value, income or emotion? The discussion we imagine at the gallery is as likely to focus on artistic movement as on the economic value of the work. However, the role of the creative economy and the creative arts in economic development is largely undervalued. In recent years, several economic development initiatives have prioritised housing stock, business development, and been driven by complex governance delivery arrangements. This book is about the role of the creative arts, both as a creative sector of industry and as community-facing creative arts groups, in the governance of economic development and renewal projects. It examines the ways in which the creative sector, and the creative arts more broadly, engage in projects that work with their local community or area in development and regeneration projects that target youth or social engagement, and are engaged with the community through governance mechanisms, networks, funding projects and engagement. The creative sector, and its role in economic development, is looked at and the behaviours of actors engaged in these initiatives are examined.

Three national comparative case studies across the UK, Canada and Germany are drawn on, and a global chapter offering an overview of comparative cases and best and worst practice (that is, projects meeting targets) and a chapter detailing the linkage between theory and practice, providing summaries of best practice and the key points of governance structure, funding mechanisms and partnerships, are included. This book is about the role of creative economy groups in the governance of economic development projects.

Much of the existing canvas of literature that examines the role of the creative arts and the creative economy in driving and delivering economic development tends to focus on city, region or nation case studies, rather than exploring learning across comparative studies. Moreover, the existing scope of the scholarly debates on this topic do seem to have focused for the most part on the role of the creative economy in economic development in rather splendid isolation. To be sure, there are aspects of the literature that do address the role of the creative economy and the environment in driving economic development and related sustainability initiatives across a range of subnational cases, which are detailed in depth in the following chapter. This book, however, moves this debate forward by producing new knowledge. We argue that the role of the creative economy in economic development does indeed overlap with that of environmentalism and sustainability; but moreover, it is also overlapping and interwoven with the visitor economy. It brings new knowledge in examining the effects of the creative arts and the creative economy in driving economic development. They have the potential, conceptually, to disrupt established notions of structure and agency, nudge and behaviourism in advancing the scholarly debate.

This book represents a new contribution and adds new knowledge to established and existing literature in three main ways: (i) first, it examines a policy area of significant importance, both in terms of economic development and also broader political economy issues such as inclusivity, mobility, funding and employment; (ii) second, it achieves this through the comparative context, drawing on case-study examples in the UK, Germany and Canada; (iii) third, it examines these cases using the behavioural approach set out above, rather than a comparison of regional difference, funding alone, or a top-down institutionalism or party-politics approach. The book disrupts existing conceptual understandings of economic development and governance theory such as behavioural governance, structure and agency, and nudge approaches by focusing on a key area of moving policy space, a key social and economic area of focus for multiple levels of governance, as well as then examining this in comparative context. This book brings new knowledge in crucial policy arenas to both conceptual and practical debates at regional, national and global levels.

In terms of key themes, the book comes from a behavioural governance perspective conceptually, but one of its main objectives is to contribute to a range of literatures. The sustainability focus of the work means the work will contribute to political economy, public policy, politics and geography debates, as well as planning and sociology. The book seeks to examine debates around sustainability, regeneration and governance and looks at case studies in the UK, Germany and Canada as well as including a global chapter offering an overview of best practice (that is, projects meeting targets) and a chapter detailing the relationship between theory and practice. The book examines the ways in which creative arts organisations are engaged with their local community or area in projects that target youth, older people, mental and physical wellbeing, rehabilitation health or fostering social engagement. The book draws upon the behavioural approach in governance to examine the roles these creative arts groups play in governance partnerships, projects and networks in funding, engagement and delivery with regeneration programmes across the three case-study areas.

Since antiquity, art has been used to campaign for and against, politicise, parody and portray governments and political change. For Andre Malraux, art was 'a revolt against fate'; stages and schools of art in different nations have charted and pushed for political change, such as the shock of the new; and community renewal projects have drawn upon the creative arts in a much more micro sense, using art forms such as graffiti or street arts, sculpture or installation, or the use of painting, drawing, writing or music as forms of art therapy for rehabilitation. This book focuses on the role of creative arts organisations in urban renewal and community projects, as part of the governance of these projects. The book is focused on the ways creative arts organisations and projects engage with communities to foster economic development and renewal, drawing upon case studies from the UK, Germany and Canada. The UK case study examines the role of Take A Part (TAP), a creative arts organisation; the Canadian case examines the Creative Cities Network; and the German chapter examines the role of Creative Renewal in economic development.

Each of these case-study chapters examines the ways in which these organisations have worked with local communities, as well as a range of other collaborators, such as, for example, local levels of governance and businesses. The role of creative arts organisations and the wider creative economy in fostering economic development has been driven by the use of visual arts projects, partnerships with a range of actors, galleries and exhibitions, and performances. Moreover, of course, these activities overlap with other important economic sectors such as the visitor economy, knowledge economy and sports economy in driving economic development. For example, do we characterise a music festival or a football match that attracts tourism to a city as creative activity, or sports, or visitor economy? The longer-term sustainability of these projects is evidently subject to wider political issues, notably substantial cuts to funding for creative arts organisations, community groups and local governments, and – as will be set out in detail in Chapter 3 – is examined through the comparative behavioural governance approach.

A note on key terms and their use

Throughout this book, the terms creative sector, creative arts and creative economy are used. These are key terms in understanding the role of creative practices and organisations in economic development initiatives. Though different terms that apply to different contexts, the importance of both the creative economy – through digital media, small and medium enterprise (SME) development and longer-term goals such as education and training, or technological development – and the creative arts each have a vital role to play in underpinning economic development initiatives, through aspects such as SME development, community engagement, job creation and the visibility of economic development in areas.

Case-study selection

The book focuses on the three cases of the UK, Germany and Canada. These cases have been selected because they each represent examples of subnational economic development initiatives that have been driven by the creative arts and the creative economy. In some cases, these are aspects of the design of the economic development initiative, while in others they are bottom-up, more grassroots, organisations that have driven economic development in the case-study areas. The cases, and their selection, are addressed in more depth in Chapter 3. The literature has established debates, set out in the following chapter, around the importance of the creative arts and the broader creative economy as a grassroots mechanism for community politics.

Comparative approach

This book brings new knowledge through examining cases using the behavioural approach, in comparative context. The behavioural governance focus across the cases examines the role of nudge and the roles of, and the relations between, various actors involved in the design and delivery, and the success, of economic development initiatives. The comparative focus also examines the potential for differences and constraints driven by governance and institutional design, and the effects these may have on the behaviours of actors across the cases.

Chapter synopsis

Chapter 1 The creative arts in governance of urban renewal and development

This chapter sets the context for the key debates and questions that concern the book in terms of creative arts and renewal initiatives globally, drawn both from the academic literatures and from the grey practice literature. This chapter examines the role of governance mechanisms and projects in a broad global context, before focusing on each of the national-level case studies. These organisations have undertaken economic development projects, been responsible for community engagement within them, and have set targets and funding levels, linked to economic development initiatives and are examined in detail across national, regional and local levels in the empirical national case-study chapters. This represents one of the key contributions of the book, advancing the academic literature and the conceptual approaches of governance, arguing that the behaviours of both top-down creative economy policies from national governments and community-based programmes each achieve renewal through the creative sector.

Chapter 2 Creative sector and economic development: governance, funding and delivery

This chapter summarises the academic literatures and the grey literatures, focusing on creative arts projects, renewal and governance. The existing academic debates around the role of communities and governance mechanisms driven by creative arts initiatives are examined, and contrasted with local, regional and national discussions of renewal. The chapter then moves on to summarise the relevant, historical and recent debates around governance as a framework or method from both academic and practice sources. As noted in the initial sections of the proposal above, the existing literatures and debates that have focused on the creative economy and economic development were driven by subnational or single-country analysis. Moreover, these debates have focused on the role of the creative economy in driving economic development in isolation. We contend that the role of the creative economy in economic development is a more complex beast than this would suggest. The role of, for example, environmentalism and sustainability has been documented to an extent, but not in terms of the expansion of the green economy, nor in a comparative context. Moreover, we argue here that there is also significant potential for overlap with the visitor economy. Behavioural governance also underpins our comparative cross-national approach theoretically. This is vital in interrogating the roles of different actors, organisations and institutions in the design and delivery of economic development initiatives that are driven by the roles of creative economy organisations and communities.

Chapter 3 Governance and institutional context: policy, behaviour and communities

This chapter examines and applies the key governance approaches and models to the case-study areas, setting up a governance model which draws upon the frameworks of behaviourism (inter alia, John, 2017; Sorensen, 2013, 2012, 2006, 2002; Bevir and Rhodes, 2006; Bevir, 2005), and can be applied and tested in economic development programmes at local, regional or national level. In this way, the project advances the academic literature and the conceptual approaches of governance, each linked to practice. The interpretive behavioural approach to governance emphasises the key tensions and relations between key actors in the political economy of economic development programmes: who is funding; what is the relationship between specific projects in the case studies and the wider strategic aims of the funding programme; where does power lie; where does cooperation occur; what are the short- and long-term effects of the investment, politically and economically? In examining the relationships between these actors and drawing upon the behavioural approach, the book focuses on the successes or failures of the creative sector in economic development across local, regional, national and supranational levels. National-level governments and community-facing groups have each undertaken projects, focused on community engagement, targets and funding levels as part of economic development initiatives. These are the focus of the empirical national case study chapters. The method employed within the behavioural approach will be three-fold: first, analysis of funding streams in prior and current projects; second, analysis of progress of economic development initiatives in the case-study areas, data on spend and funding partnerships; and third, analysis of datasets in the funded areas. The relationship between these actors is examined drawing upon the behavioural approach. The chapter then moves on to set out the methodological design and approach of the book, taking the behavioural approach set out in this chapter, and applies the conceptual contribution of the book within theoretical paradigms. The post-positivist approach of the book, using the behavioural governance perspective, is set out before discussing the conceptual contribution of the book. These sections of the chapter focus on the institutional effect on behavioural governance, in terms of institutional design across the cases, nationally, regionally and locally; and also, theoretically, examine the potential for disruption to theory, in particular to established debates around behaviouralism, paternalism and nudge.

Chapter 4 UK: Take A Part

This chapter examines the role of Take A Part, a creative arts organisation in the UK, linking creative arts organisations in the regeneration programme, working in partnership with regional and national governing bodies, and examines the issue of these actors in delivering events, working with businesses and communities, taking on the role of governance, alongside the state. The projects focus on connecting creative arts in the various regeneration projects, acting as a focus of governance, drawing in partners in delivery from the creative arts sector. The chapter examines the progress of the projects, the relations between actors, and the goals and progress of regeneration projects and delivery from the creative economy sector.

- What does the role of the creative economy mean in terms of accountability?
- What about notions of a governance gap?

- Are these organisations different? Are they responsible or formally representative of communities; unelected; or a corporate or a third sector organisation?
- Informal governance (Ayres, 2017).
- Are they 'filling in the governance gap' of the local level and third sector?
- Are there implications for accountability or legitimacy?
- Governance roles and behaviours?
- ' Ad hoc' rather than formal delivery driven by behaviours?
- Disrupting governance theory?
- Austerity versus 'Best Value Management' (Stoker, 2016)
- Does this relate to the idea of 'informal governance' (Ayres, 2017)?
- Reframing structure and agency, and the role of nudge?

Chapter 5 Germany: from creative and cultural industries to Refugees' Kitchen

This chapter examines the role of the Creative Renewal programme in Germany, linking creative arts organisations in the regeneration programmes. The chapter then focuses on the role of Creative Renewal and its role in governance, working in partnership with regional and national governing bodies, and investigates the issue of these actors in delivering events, working with businesses and communities, taking on the role of governance, alongside the state. The projects focus on connecting and coordinating the various creative arts regeneration projects, acting as a focus of governance, drawing in partners in delivery from the creative arts sector. The chapter focuses on the progress of the projects, the relations between actors and the linkage between governance and the creative arts in regeneration.

- What does the role of the creative economy mean in terms of accountability?
- What about notions of a governance gap?
- Are these organisations different? Are they responsible or formally representative of communities; unelected; or a corporate or a third sector organisation?
- Informal governance (Ayres, 2017).
- Are they 'filling in the governance gap' of the local level and third sector?
- Are there implications for accountability or legitimacy?
- Governance roles and behaviours?
- 'Ad hoc' rather than formal delivery driven by behaviours?
- Disrupting governance theory?
- Austerity versus 'Best Value Management' (Stoker, 2016).

- Does this relate to the idea of 'informal governance' (Ayres, 2017)?
- Reframing structure and agency, and the role of nudge?

Chapter 6 Canada: the Creative Inter Cities Network to Artscape

This chapter examines the role of the Creative Cities Network, working with creative arts organisations and regional and national governance tiers. The role of the Creative Cities Network and the creative arts more broadly as key partners in the delivery and governance of regeneration projects is examined in this chapter that draws upon the behavioural approach to unpack the roles the creative arts organisations play in governance of these regeneration projects. The projects focus on connecting and coordinating the various creative arts regeneration projects, acting as a focus of governance, drawing in partners in delivery from the creative arts sector. The chapter focuses on the progress of the projects, the relations between actors and the linkage between governance and creative arts in regeneration, and investigates the issue of these actors in delivering events, working with businesses and communities, taking on the role of governance, alongside the state. The projects focus on connecting the creative economy in the various economic development projects. The complexities of governance delivery arrangements, such as the use of partners in delivery from the creative economy sector, may also act a disincentive to engage communities in the creative arts (Sorensen, 2012, 2006). The chapter examines the roles of both tiers of governance and communities in the projects, the relations between these actors and the role of the creative economy as a driver in the governance of these economic development projects.

- What does the role of the creative economy mean in terms of accountability?
- What about notions of a governance gap?
- Are these organisations different? Are they responsible or formally representative of communities; unelected; or a corporate or a third sector organisation?
- Informal governance (Ayres, 2017).
- Are they 'filling in the governance gap' of the local level and third sector?
- Are there implications for accountability or legitimacy?
- Governance roles and behaviours?
- 'Ad hoc' rather than formal delivery driven by behaviours?
- Disrupting governance theory?
- Austerity versus 'Best Value Management' (Stoker, 2016).
- Does this relate to the idea of 'informal governance' (Ayres, 2017)?
- Reframing structure and agency, and the role of nudge?

Chapter 7 Comparing across the creative sector:
governance, best practice and communities

This concluding chapter begins by identifying themes of good practice across the case studies, before then examining and revisiting the challenges posed by economic development initiatives, funding, community engagement, and institutional levers and governance mechanisms in these empirical studies. Having made these conclusions, the chapter then moves on to identify future comparative case studies looking at the creative economy in economic development and governance. This chapter examines and unpacks the key themes across both theory and practice, and the potential for overlap with the visitor and green economies, drawn from an overview of a range of economic development projects engaged with governance, investigating the contribution to the literature and to governance theory, as well as summarising the contribution to practice made by the book, and how these two contributions interlink.

Finally, the chapter returns to the importance of the behavioural approach. In applying this framework, the book has examined the roles of actors, nudges, power relations and networks across the three subnational case-study areas. Key to the understanding of the role of the creative economy in economic development for regional, national and global governance institutions is the importance of understanding behaviours locally and regionally in terms of governance, and across businesses and communities. Unpacking the motivations that drive behaviours (such as participation in the creative sector) that effect success of economic development initiatives, and understanding the power relations and roles between actors, are vital.

Chapter 8 The creative sector and economic development:
global cases, next steps and reframing theory

This concluding chapter revisits the key research questions set out in the book, and compares across the cases. Focusing on the key themes and findings of the book, the chapter examines the conceptual meanings that arise from the case study chapters. The focus of the book on behavioural governance will be revisited here, and the conceptual importance of the cases in terms of governance will be investigated.

Conclusions

This introductory chapter has set out the key aims and approach of the book. The book proceeds as follows. As discussed in the sections above, the book focuses on the role of behaviours between actors in the creative economy and the role of the creative economy in economic development. More broadly, the governance around the creative economy and economic development is unpacked in terms of behaviours. The different aspects of governance investigated across all the cases in this book, namely the importance of legitimacy, accountability, fragmentation, delivery and funding, are examined in the context of the creative economy and its role in economic development initiatives. The book represents the first comparative study of cross-national cases of the creative economy and its role in economic development. In addition, the conceptual contribution of the book is to deliver new knowledge in behaviourism and related underpinning ideas of structure and agency. The book aims to do this by focusing on the behaviours of actors in the creative economy, and if and how these organisations affect economic development initiatives across the three case-study areas.

We now move on to addressing and unpacking the established scholarly and practice debates around the creative economy, if and how the creative economy relates to wider economic development initiatives, and the conceptual debates around behaviourism, structure and agency, and the comparative behavioural approach. The book then moves on to investigating the three case-study areas in detail across the empirical chapters, before the final chapter examines the key findings, and the global relevance of these. The book concludes by revisiting the conceptual contribution of the book, further research and limitations of the research.

References

Ayres, S. (2017) Assessing the impact of informal governance on political innovation *Public Management Review* 19 (1): 90–107

Bevir, M. (2005) *New labour: A critique* Abingdon: Routledge

Bevir, M. and Rhodes, R. A. W. (2006) The life, death and resurrection of British governance *Australian Journal of Public Administration* 65 (2): 59–69

John, P. (2017) *How far to nudge? Assessing behavioural public policy* Cheltenham: Edward Elgar

Sorensen, E. (2002) Democratic theory and network governance *Administrative Theory & Praxis* 24 (4): 693–720

Sorensen, E. (2006) Metagovernance: The changing role of politicians in processes of democratic governance *American Review of Public Administration* 36 (1): 98–114

Sorensen, E. (2012) Governance networks as a frame for inter-demoi participation and deliberation *Administrative Theory & Praxis* 34 (4): 509–532

Sorensen, E. (2013) Institutionalizing interactive governance for democracy *Critical Policy Studies* 7 (1): 72–86

Stoker, G. (2016) *Why politics matter: Making democracy work* London: Palgrave Macmillan

2 Creative sector and economic development

Governance, funding and delivery

What are the key debates?

This chapter focuses on the established key scholarly debates around the creative arts, creative economy and wider economic development. The chapter begins by examining the established conceptual and case study driven debates in the literature around the creative sector, economic development and the wider creative arts, and then moves on to apply these debates to those scholarly ideas that address wider economic development initiatives. The chapter then moves on to investigate the importance of the underpinning conceptual discussion, structure and agency, and the underlying tensions between institutional thought and behavioural public policy; it then examines the grey literature emerging from the comparative cases of the UK, Germany and Canada.

Creative economy

This section of the chapter focuses on the established debates on the role of the creative economy. Evidently, the creative economy umbrella is vast, encompassing areas such as art galleries, performing arts, festivals, and – as noted elsewhere in this book – often overlaps with other economic spaces such as the visitor economy; tourism and sustainability (Syamsudin and Subono, 2018); the sports economy; and the knowledge and digital economies. The creative economy also cuts across large differing sectors such as the SME sector and the cultural sector (Houston, 2019; Radomska *et al.*, 2019; Rodriques and Franco, 2019) – especially driven by established spaces of galleries and museums, and traditional niche areas of economic activity such as heritage and craft. Established debates in these areas explore the role of culture and heritage in the creative economy and the distinction between the creative industries and creative occupations (Bennett, 2018). The creative economy is also accepted in scholarly debate as overlapping substantially with the green or sports economy in some contexts, and has tended to be conceptualised as a broad range of activities. The following sections unpack the key established debates in these areas.

The notion of heritage and craft is a key area of debate in the scholarly literature, with discussions such as Bennett's (2018) work on craft and handmade aspects of the creative industries, and indeed, the problem of capturing the vast scope of the creative sector, with the issue of formal and informal definitions in the sector. These definitions may fail to capture the scale of creative activities and industries. Moreover, the importance of creative industries as a means of sharing and showcasing cultures is widely discussed in the literature. Within these debates, culture is examined in terms of innovation and thought (Malinowski and Howkins, 2018); the video gaming industry (Crogan, 2018); and broader aspects of culture and creativity in public policy-making (Paquette, 2018). Equally, these debates, which address the role of the creative economy and the creative city, flow from the global context, such as the Chinese context (Ren, 2018), the Romanian context (Suciu *et al.*, 2018), to the local. For example, the role of the creative economy has also been examined at the community level (Clements, 2018), and in terms of well-being and living choices (Florida, 2010), as has the role of the creative sector in small cities and the governance process around this (Comunian, 2011; Waitt and Gibson, 2009).

Changing political economy and public policy

Several scholars have examined the creative sector as a mechanism for driving change in living, in cities and in the types of work we undertake. The growing role of the creative industries and the development of the creative economy have also driven new ideas of how the vast range of creative industries impact on our working lives and the way we live, especially in urban contexts. This has implications for policy-making and for communities engaging in the creative sector, and for the expansion of the creative economy (Markusen and Wassall, 2008; Hartley, 2005; Howkins, 2002; Tepper, 2002).

Moreover, the expanding roles of the creative sector, and the policy implications, have created debates around workplace treatment and environments, and also the potential precarity of the creative sector. There is also the potential issue of capital flight of the 'creative class' as professionals with expertise in the creative economy or creative arts may leave an area (Florida, 2006, 2004), increased competition in the expanding global creative sector, issues arising from established power relations in the sector (Belfiore, 2018) and the policy problem of inequality in the sector or as a result of this rapid expansion; and the need to maintain management practices across the sector (Bilton and Puttnam, 2007). Moreover, there are overarching and uncomfortable questions about the lack of community engagement with politics and public life (Buller *et al*, 2019; Cerny, 1990).

Creative arts

As Markusen (2006) has argued, the role of an active and socially engaged 'creative class' acts as a means of encouraging participation among the community. The creative arts can be a major driving force in terms of both urban politics and community development, drawing on arts projects in Florida; while Ponzini and Rossi (2010) examined the role of networks and creative arts in Baltimore in achieving notions of an 'urban renaissance', working with and engaging the local community and governance actors through regenerative creative arts projects. To be sure, there is also a rich history in some cases, which annotates a community's evolving politics through the creative arts (Winegar, 2006). More broadly, the chapter contributes to discussions of community governance, regeneration and social capital, with the community as partners or leaders (inter alia, Bailey and Pill, 2015; Beebeejaun *et al.*, 2015; McKee, 2015; Seyfang and Haxeltine, 2012; Taylor, 2007; Bull and Jones, 2006; Robinson *et al.*, 2005; Bowles and Gintis, 2002; Sullivan, 2001; Purdue, 2001).

Place and creative economy

The vast literatures on place and place-making, while not the focus of this book, need to be considered and addressed. The importance of place underpins economic development strategies, and has tended to be a polarising question for communities and policy-makers alike. In terms of large urban areas where the creative industries have been successful, Hamburg and Munich have both been highly visible in terms of employment (Power, 2011) and national-level investment. The role of the creative industries as a broader driver for employment and economic growth in the German context has also been examined in detailed studies by Wiesand and Soendermann (2005), who address a comparative study of growth; while the creative industries also occupy a large space in the academic literature in terms of long-standing heritage and cultural industries (Volkerling, 2001). The role of heritage and cultural industries, such as crafts, have been examined in debates that have also addressed the role of heritage and cultural arts at the city and regional governance levels (Kunzmann, 2004).

Again, this is a broad church of creative industries encompassing both ancient crafts and innovations across technologies, both of which are united through debates around the notion of creative industries. For example, established debates such as the link between culture and creative industries and the policy goals of these approaches (Garnham, 2005) have identified tensions between the public and private sectors in driving innovation across the creative sector (Czarnitzki and Fier, 2002); how to develop the creative sector across differing nation states (Wyszomirski, 2004); and how national level policy can drive creative industries (Fjoord, 2009).

Debates have also addressed cultural policy and culture value, in terms of the policy implications for these creative sectors (Cunningham, 2002), and the problems with attempts to define such a broad church of creative activities within one large umbrella (Galloway and Dunlop, 2007). Moreover, debates have addressed the linkage between these cultural industries and the overarching policy-making that surrounds them (Miller, 2010; Hesmondhalgh and Pratt, 2005) and the resultant management techniques that have arisen in the sector (O'Brien, 2013). Equally, there is a substantial and well-established literature that addresses the role of the creative sector and creative arts more broadly in terms of creative spaces. These debates have focused on the creative arts as a means of urban politics, grass roots and a tool for urban renewal. They examine the role of the creative arts in driving the city as a creative space and place (Evans, 2009) and the consequences (certainly for economic development and renewal) of engendering a creative class in a city (Pratt, 2005).

Moreover, debates have addressed the notion of culture value, through the idea of heritage, place and also in terms of community cohesion. Evidently, the work of Bourdieu has been highly influential and debated across the literatures in terms of structure and agency (Peterson, 2019), and place and consciousness. This linkage to creativity and place is important in the agent being situated within their place and their consciousness developing in that context. The focus on structure and agency is important in underpinning these debates, though in the context of this book these debates are not centred on the individual. Rather, they are around the processes of governance and the interactions between actors inside and outside established structures and walls.

Gaps in knowledge: economic development

The roles of the creative sector, and the creative arts more broadly, have long been drivers in social change. However, a number of the established debates set out in the sections above reveal some important gaps in knowledge. First, there is a clear distinction in many of the debates between the creative arts and the creative industries. This means that the linkage between these two categories has been somewhat neglected in understanding the importance of both established creative industries and creative arts organisations in driving economic development. The often wide-ranging aims of economic development initiatives, both regionally and nationally, have focused on the importance of job creation, business development and investment. In addition, the broad church of aims that economic development often seeks to address includes raising educational attainment, green space, community engagement and social inclusion. There are examples of these aims being addressed across multiple cases and through varying means. For example, there is a bakery in Liverpool that has been driven by a need to equip young people in the area with skills and to enable greater social engagement. This type of example is also one that both contributes to the local economy and drives the more social aims of economic development, such as facilitating greater social inclusion and community engagement. The book addresses both the contribution of established creative industries – such as that driven by the small and medium enterprise (SME) sector or through foreign direct investment (FDI) – and that supported by the creative arts through organisations that are not-for-profit, not formal governance organisations and not charities.

Second, there is a gap in knowledge in terms of comparison. Though there are existing debates that focus on national creative economies, such as those discussed in earlier sections of this chapter, there is no work that examines the creative economy in a national comparative context, and none that addresses the key aspect of behaviourism in the creative economy and economic development. Drawing on the comparative perspective – as will be detailed in the following chapter – the importance of this comparison lies on two aspects. First, the role of national-level public policy that focuses on the creative sector as a means of driving economic development in terms of a training and skills base, exports and job creation. There is also, however, the vital role of creative arts organisations which engage with communities at street level, often with broad remits around social change and development driven through the means of the creative arts. The book will examine these problems and the implications they have for governance, practically and conceptually.

Behavioural public policy

The underpinning conceptual debates in this book on institutions and governance will be more detailed in the following chapter, though there is a large and emerging literature on these themes. The role of changes in behaviour is key to economic development initiatives, and is also vital in achieving successful policy change. The role of behaviour has been documented in scholarly debates that have addressed a range of policy arenas such as health, the environment and transport, and the role of behaviour change (and through nudge, which is addressed in subsequent sections of this chapter) is key to achieving successful policy and wider economic development initiatives. In terms of the creative arts and the creative economy, often these are aspects of economic development that mean wholescale and rapid changes to employment, communities or even the physical landscape in an area. These changes risk influencing behaviour in a negative way: perhaps through the pace of change itself or the lack of visibility or engagement in implementing and delivering the economic development initiative. The creative economy might also mean a different set of neighbours, different job opportunities in an area, and might also exacerbate perceived ideas of difference among communities. The emphasis on green space and health, or education, as key aspects of economic development initiatives has also involved changing behaviours.

Nudge

The notion of nudge as a basis for policy-making has been documented in depth by some scholars (John, 2017; John *et al.*, 2009) and lies in its ability to foster behaviour change through policy. The success and extent of nudge has been well documented in practice, driven by the Behavioural Insights Team (BIT) in UK central government, and by related high-profile policies such as those that address health issues. Notably, such policies have tackled long-standing health issues and have been extremely high profile: the 10,000 steps; the five-a-day fruit and vegetable campaign; and aspects of green policy, such as recycling. The intricacies of nudge thinking, however, lie in the strength of the nudge. The policies above are subject to intense debate around the role of personal freedoms, the reach of the state and the liberty of individuals – their freedom to make the wrong choice, as it were. John (2017) argues the subtlety of the nudge is the key to success in these policies. The more subtle the nudge, the greater the chance of success.

We can contrast this with policies in these spaces that were designed to alter behaviour and affect change, such as the smoking ban in public places that came into force in July 2007, or the 5 pence levy on plastic bags. These were shifts in policy rather than nudges, though each contains aspects of the types of behaviour change that are outlined in economic development initiatives, such as greener behaviours and healthier lifestyles. Additionally, the roles of the creative economy and the creative arts are often bound up with nudges. The role of established creative industries, like the galleries and museums discussed in the initial stages of this chapter, has been a key focus of behaviour change through attempts to attract a broader and more diverse audience through their doors. To critics of this approach, who emphasise the individual liberty of individuals to be free from the interference of paternalism, these represent attempts to direct behaviour change through nudge to direct the courses of individuals' lives towards top-down prescribed policy outcomes. The agency of individuals has been, for liberals, limited by attempts to change behaviour towards healthier lifestyles, greener behaviours or, in the instance examined in this book, participation in creative arts.

Agency

Turning to utilitarian thought, the emphasis is on harm, interference and the moral and just right of the individual to pursue their own freedom. At first glance, the tensions between a policy focus on individualism and the concomitant effects on social justice are highly problematic. Of course, this argument is as much about resources as social justice. However, drawing on the utilitarian perspective in protecting individual choice, and emphasising freedom, the individual has a duty, as John Stuart Mill suggests, to ensure that the individual's pursuit of freedoms and desires does not harm others in *their* pursuit of freedoms. Following Mill, older individuals who choose to extend their working lives could potentially exercise harm on younger people by excluding them from the labour market in increasing competition. However, this is a question of resources, rather than solely justice and individual freedom. Governments have a duty to ensure that competition is accessible to all age groups in the labour market.

The consequentialist thinkers have tended to focus on the way policy outcomes react to perceived 'behavioural' aspects of individuals. The subsequent debates around just policy design centre upon perverse incentives of a complex state, and policies that have been argued to reward the five welfare giants rather than to reduce them. The focus on life and financial situation as a result of personal effort and ability is a consistent theme in the arguments of consequentialist thinkers such as Hayek, Friedman and Murray. Consequentialists such as Nozick (1974) suggest governments construct notions of need and reward to gain electoral advantage. Hayek's notion of a minimum state or deregulated markets (sometimes mistakenly conflated with 'free' markets) has tended to be discussed through the lens of inequality, and to be sure, examples from recent history demonstrate that governments have induced these effects by retreating from provision. However, the justification for these actions by the state has been framed as prioritising individualism and emphasising personal responsibility. For surely, the treatment of need as a binary choice for policy-makers between rewarding the few and a broader redistribution is false. The fact that the policy-makers and states have, in large part, presented this binary choice as an awkward reality to individuals, has singly frustrated debate on the role of need and social justice. However, the notion of need as a scale is an idea examined by Hayek in his critique of central planning and state determinism:

> The social goal or common purpose for which society is to be organised, is usually vaguely described as the common good, or the general welfare, or the general interest. The Hayekian objection is not the extent of planning, rather the ideas and objectives of planning. The idea of a scale or hierarchy of needs that Hayek alludes to in his theory suggests the need for a new approach to the construction of morality discussed in the earlier sections of this article. The state cannot continue to construct (and, for Hayek, impose) morality in discussions of need. What Hayek advocates in fact is a much different conception of morality, which is not constructed by the state but rather which allows for points of difference and moral objection to be made by individuals.
>
> (Hayek, 1945: 65– 67)

Where people's economic wellbeing is the paramount concern, consequentialists insist that voluntary exchange is preferable to the coercive intrusion of public institutions. Negative rights must be prioritised, not because they are consistent with universal attributes of human nature – such as the capacity for conscious deliberation and sovereign action – but because their enforcement sustains the institutions that are able to maximise welfare. But, at the same time, this emphasis on the importance of outcomes suggests that liberty may be sacrificed where this might reasonably be expected to yield greater utility. Crucially, this means that statutory measures to circumscribe voluntary exchange 'must be evaluated on their merits rather than rejected *apriori* on natural rights grounds' (Friedman, 1989/2016: 173). Herbert Spencer's discomfort with the machinery of government is, he argues, a major reason for the failures of representation (1982). The issue of representation is problematic because the component parts of government (and, by extension, to an even greater extent in layers of *governance*) are overly complex. Applying Spencer to the problem of needs, the size and staffing of governments is especially problematic, as these institutions take and construct morality of the individual, rather than represent moralities. Spencer argues that the complex machinery of government reduces the chances of effectiveness and also of individuals' needs being met in a just fashion.

The role of the state

Let us suppose, for a moment, that the limits of governments are understood plainly: that this machinery cannot eradicate social need or the basest and most desperate conditions in favour of more productive, financially rewarding and fulfilling lives; that the scope for policy-making is radically framed, just as in a tribute musical act, by what has gone before and proven popular; and that the debate surrounding need and social justice must inevitably favour the individual or the collective. These, as such, are the limits of policy. The rational focus of governments, then, must be to keep the majority of the population somewhat satisfied, rather than happy – a vast umbrella of comfortable disquiet labelled 'consensus', which seeks to embrace those who wish to cast off limits on individual freedom and those who wish to extend redistribution. This framework of limited agency and choice echoes much of the thought of Spencer, particularly in his discussions of over-legislation and of the role of representative government. These discussions are no nearer to being resolved or finding consensus, in the current modern social and political era:

> Though we no longer presume to coerce men for their *spiritual good*, we still think ourselves called upon to coerce them for their *material good*: not seeing that the one is as useless and as unwarrantable as the

other ... Take up a daily paper and you will probably find a leader exposing the corruption, negligence, or mismanagement of some State-department. Cast your eye down the next column, and it is not unlikely that you will read proposals for an extension of State-supervision.

(Spencer, 1982: 268)

Such withering observations are found daily in the discussions of need, and in policy which has tended to veer between the kind that Spencer criticises here, such as high levels of investment in complex, hard-to-navigate policies; or the kind of moral emphasis that has been used as justification to roll back spending on the basis that needs are the results and outcomes of individuals' respective choices (on matters such as savings, diet, health and lifestyle). Though each of these arguments has much justification to support it, the issue is not only the readiness of governments to be either paternalistic or moralistic; rather it is the framework through which they (and, therefore necessarily, society) must view needs. As different as these approaches to policy may be, each, however, emphasises the involuntary contribution of every adult individual in society. Why is this question such a vital point? Because, as the previous sections highlight, policy-makers have tended overwhelmingly to view need as a lens or consequence of too much or too little engineering of social justice: the paternalists see the need to invest in policy responses to social inequality; while market-oriented Conservatives (though not emphasising a free market) have sought to reduce spending and encourage individuals to be entrepreneurial and competitive, and self-reliant. However, the problem with such divergent perspectives of social justice and need is that while they may consider the role of the state vis-à-vis a group of people or even a demographic group, or geographic area, neither of these approaches considers properly the role of need in terms of the *individual* and the state. Let us pause here. This chapter is not suggesting that, simply, individuals should be self-reliant and that this forms the basis of policies, which deal with need. States have a responsibility to ensure a safety net of a minimum standard of living; but these debates are also challenged by the actions of states. It should also be stressed that, as Spencer suggests, these are not problems driven by traditional left–right division; but rather they are more entrenched and complex, and can be viewed as a manifestation of what King and Crewe (2013) have referred to as 'the blunders of our governments'.

Structure, institutional design and governance delivery

The roles of institutions and the resultant scholarly debates around structure and agency are underpinning ideas in the creative sector. The role of governance across the creative sector and the fundamental notions of institutional design are embedded in ideas around the related concepts of structure and agency. These long-standing and wide-ranging debates have focused on the tensions between institutional structures and agents, and the friction between these aspects of governance. The discussion elsewhere in this chapter that focuses on liberty and the role of the state in changing behaviour though public policy is key to the role of structure and agency. The debates are also addressed in the following chapter on philosophical and methodological design. Recent debates in this area of scholarly debates have focused on the role of the spatial nature of structure and agency (Forde, 2019); the informal influence of work in urban living as a type of structure or agency (Lombard, 2019); and the role of agency in informing societal and scholarly debates in our understandings of political behaviour (Akram, 2019). Equally, scholars have discussed the role of free will and determinism as underpinning ideals of structure and agency (Pleasants, 2019), and in the creative context, the importance of structure and agency tensions (Silliman, 2001). Moreover, the comparative context of this book draws upon the global nature of the structure–agency debate across a variety of institutions and governance settings and examines disruptions to long-established ideas (Friedmann and Starr, 2002; Wendt, 1995; Moe, 1989; Castles, 1981).

UK: the creative sector and Take A Part

The UK focus on the creative sector and the importance of investment in the creative economy (investigated in depth in Chapter 4) has been a significant aspect of the UK Government's industrial strategy. The core policy priorities emphasised within the UK's *Creative Sector Industrial Strategy* of investment, employment and training reflect longer-term growth in terms of the creative economy. The strategy draws together several strands of the creative sector as policy priorities for investment and growth. These include the need for regional distribution of funding, skills and employment, and the need to invest in existing areas of strength. There is a focus on the role of exports in the creative sector, with the creative economy worth £84.1 billion to the UK economy in 2018 (Department for Culture, Media and Sport (DCMS), 2018). These targeted areas clearly aim to deliver increased skills, training and more distributed funding for the creative sector and the arts more broadly across regions. As identified in the introductory chapter, there is a rupture within the broad scope of the creative sector, through two sides of the debate. There are both top-down and bottom-up dimensions to debates around the creative sector, and these will be examined in the theoretical and methodological debates in the next chapter, as well as in the empirical case-study chapters.

Box 2.1 Take A Part

About Take A Part

Take A Part are experts in socially engaged audience development for contemporary art.

Based in Plymouth we work in areas of socio-economic deprivation and regeneration that don't usually engage in the arts.

Our long-term, embedded process starts with listening and supporting communities to set agendas for projects that reflect and address community need and diversity. There is a great interest in our work because our genuine processes with communities leads us to co-commissioning exceptional national and international artists in those communities.

We embed contemporary arts practice in the process of regeneration, and paramount to the process is the fact that the process of creating the work itself is as important as what is created. Our purpose is to engage, educate and inform new audiences in contemporary arts while developing policy and setting agendas for neighbourhood regeneration initiatives in Plymouth. Take A Part's work contributes directly to the social infrastructure of the city.

Take A Part started in 2006 in Efford, Plymouth as a series of pilot projects supporting the area's regeneration. Engaging residents in contemporary art processes allowed for deep and creative feed into the regeneration of the area and supported the core aims of the Efford Master Plan by supporting health, young people, skills development, access to green space and physical changes to place.

By 2011 Take A Part had grown, working in other areas of the city, and by 2014 we began to work regionally and nationally to support other organisations, advocate for socially engaged practice and spread our reach.

In 2016 we launched the UK's first biennial symposium on socially engaged practice, Social Making, establishing ourselves as leaders of socially engaged practice in the South West region and since then, we have developed a successful line of consultancy and partnership commissions across the UK and internationally, supporting local authorities, arts organisations, educational institutions etc to widen their audience reach.

We have been awarded the prestigious Arts Council England National Portfolio Status for the 2018–2022 period, securing our programme for Plymouth.

We have fulfilled 26 commissions, organised hundreds of workshops and events, engaged 60,000 people directly and have created work that has been broadcast and been seen city-wide by 300,000 audience members.

The Efford community, our heart and home, was registered as the fifth most deprived in Plymouth when Take A Part started its pilot work in 2006. Currently, Efford now ranks as the twelfth most deprived area of the city (www.plymouth.gov.uk/nhpefford.pdf).

History

In partnership with Heart of Efford Community Partnership, Plymouth City Council and Plymouth Arts Centre the project continued to grow and in 2009 appointed a Community Curator to deliver a deeper co-commissioning process with the Efford community, supported by an Arts Action Group made up of residents, local businesses, councillors, arts professionals and the local authority.

The Take A Part process was so highly regarded and successful that in 2011, Take A Part decided to share the 'Efford experience' across the city in a series of commissions to develop interest and support new community groups to undertake their own arts initiatives.

Moving on

From 2009 to 2011 new projects were devised and delivered in collaboration with residents. Efford FM, Grow Efford, Magic Hour and Crazy Glue were established and the project was embedded in and reflected the local area, its ambitions and the agenda of the Master Plan.

By 2011, the dedication, excitement, skill and enthusiasm of the Efford area was high and the community named themselves 'Efford: The Capital of Culture for Plymouth', and worked to share their process with the rest of the city of Plymouth.

Take A Part piloted work in three other communities – Barne Barton, North Prospect and Whitleigh – whilst retaining its core work and grassroots development within Efford. Large-scale commissions reflected this stage of work with Nowhereisland Radio, In Praise of Trees, Shed On Wheels and Crazy Glue Does British Art Show 7, all engaging communities city-wide to investigate their communities, engage in art, see something new and think about change.

Crazy Glue at British Art Show 7, London

We marched, we broadcast, we sculpted, gave tours, listened to people and shared opinions. We created legacy commissions that developed pride and ownership.

And now, we are Take A Part CIC. An organisation of curators, artists, community groups, councillors and activists all supporting the need for more and better socially engaged practice.

Protesting as a part of the Take A Part exhibition 'Efford the Capital of Culture for Plymouth'

Our vision and approach

The Take A Part vision is for individuals and communities to be free to identify and realise their creative potential.

Take A Part are a significant socially engaged contemporary arts organisation that works directly with communities in a long-term process of engagement. We work on co-commissioning, co-curating and co-creating work that underpins regeneration initiatives and supports legacy. We work on creative projects with a purpose with communities, to produce socially engaged art that addresses needs and sets agendas.

The Efford community is the origin of the Take A Part process. The community have invested in arts practice and used art as a tool for regeneration and change since 2006. Here local resident, and one of the founders of Take

A Part, Michael Bridgwater shares his insights into the nature of the Efford community.

'"When you retire," said my better-off friends, patronisingly, "you can sell your little house in Efford and move to somewhere nice, maybe out in the countryside." To which my reply was, "Not a chance. I'm here where I really want to stay. Why on earth should I move?"

'How little my friends understood about life in our community. OK, some years ago the area had a reputation for being a bit wild – a bit rough around the edges; there were issues of vandalism, alcohol and drug abuse, and the occasional confrontation between the Efford Boot Boys and their counterparts in Swilly; but by and large families in the neighbourhood looked after one another and were proud to be living on top of the highest hill in the city, even if most Plymothians knew it only for the Cemetery and Crematorium.

'In the 1930s my father used to come here from Devonport for Sunday walks "in the open country" – enjoying the views out towards the moor, the river estuary and Saltram, and (being an engineer) the Great Western Railway depot down at Laira. Now Efford is largely built up – some 2000 and more homes, mostly since the Second World War – but the views are still there, as well as a very high proportion of green spaces and woodland right on our doorstep.

'Towards the end of the century the neighbourhood had become neglected and run-down, our pub – The Royal Marine – and most of the shops on Torridge Way had gone out of business. Efford Secondary School and local sports facilities closed – to become new housing estates. Both primary schools were struggling with worn-out and unsuitable buildings. Out on the edge of the city, it seemed nobody knew we were here; the world was passing us by.

'Then, after years of lobbying, came the Building Communities Initiative – to put the heart back into the centre of the Efford neighbourhood. From the start, local people had a big say in every aspect of what went on, particularly identifying and addressing the needs of young people, of more healthy living, developing our green spaces – especially the Valley – and promoting better employment and social opportunities.

'This led to the Take A Part community arts programme for more and more people of all ages to get involved in an ever-wider range of events and activities, all alongside physical improvements along and around Torridge Way – High View School, St Paul's Church, St Paul's Court and Efford Library, new housing in place of Paternoster House and, soon, on the site of the Royal Marine pub, and in Unity Park opposite the Cemetery.

'What a change! Now why should I ever want to live anywhere other than here in Efford!'

Source: www.effordtakeapart.org.uk/about/, 2019

Germany

In the German context, there is again a broad definition of the creative sector encompassing aspects of creative industries such as the gaming industry, heritage, the role of exports and investment in the digital industries. These are anchored, in the Berlin context, in the 2030 vision for the city. This strategy focuses on developing existing strength in the creative sector across Berlin and in extending these activities to wider communities. The creative sector is not seen in splendid isolation but rather is embedded in a broader narrative around strategic policy goals that focus on job creation, green living and growth.

Canada

The Canadian context also shows a large amount of grey literature, driven by several creative arts organisations that act as enablers for communities

---

Box 2.2 Innovation in Berlin

Berlin continues to follow its course of stable growth. The presence of highly innovative sectors and businesses that make Berlin a seal of quality recognised throughout Germany and the world is a key factor in ensuring economic competitiveness at the international level. Strong economic growth makes Berlin, with its sustainable and structurally sound foundation, the leading start-up city in Europe. These developments have a particularly positive knock-on effect on Berlin's jobs market. People have work, integration into the mainstream jobs market is a priority and formerly disadvantaged groups receive active support at all career levels. Berlin 2030 is greatly enhanced as a business location by the influx of talented individuals from around the world, skilled workers and entrepreneurs who boost innovation and promote international networking. Berlin has a particularly important role as the leading smart city in Europe, taking a sustainability-based approach that brings economic advantages for the regional economy and improves quality of life for its citizens. Berlin also wields international influence through its universities, colleges and research centres. The significance and reputation of Berlin's scientific and research establishments are well established. They provide attractive conditions for innovation, research and study, which are highly prized in the international community. Another of Berlin's vital strengths is in the field of technology transfer, through which the ideas generated by research are converted successfully into products and work. This is possible thanks to close links between research, business and local government, which foster progress and value creation in the region through joint innovations, thereby indirectly contributing to budget consolidation.

Source: www.stadtentwicklung.berlin.de/planen/stadtentwicklungskonzept
/download/strategie/BerlinStrategie_Broschuere_en.pdf, 2019

Box 2.3 Artscape

In 2007, Artscape embarked on a five-year plan heralding a bold new period of expansion. At the time, the Wychwood Barns was a crumbling building that had been mostly idle for close to 30 years, the Queen West Triangle was a hotbed of controversy, the Shaw Street School was empty and becoming increasingly derelict, and while the Regent Park revitalisation was getting underway, the plan lacked a place for culture.

Those unfamiliar with Artscape's dogged determination to make great things happen may have doubted the odds of transforming these challenging prospects into dynamic and award-winning creative places, especially in the midst of a deep recession and global financial crisis. Yet these projects and many other elements of the plan were brought to fruition, and with them a stronger sense of shared purpose was forged and a new appreciation for the power of 'thinking big' was born.

Our new strategic plan, Vision 2017, continues the tradition of elevating Artscape's aspirations for the future. It has been developed through two years of research and dialogue and honed by a committee of diverse stakeholders. The plan sets out four major goals and the strategic directions and key initiatives we will undertake to advance them. From this document, Artscape boards and staff have developed detailed annual work plans and performance measures to monitor success.

Perhaps the most notable shift in Vision 2017 is a determination to move beyond the noble but modest objective of helping creative people to survive the challenges of the real estate market. In the future, we will aim to create the conditions for them to thrive, something that will require new understanding and a strong sense of shared responsibility between all stakeholders.

Artscape has many exciting plans for the future, from dramatically expanding the organisation's property portfolio to solidifying our reputation as a global leader in creative place-making. Our confidence in launching this ambitious strategy is rooted in our well-developed understanding of the power of art and culture to generate value. We look forward to collaborating with our numerous Artscape communities, governments, partners, donors, investors, community leaders, clients and city-builders far and wide to realise this plan. Together we will continue to build a strong and innovative organisation that will make Toronto proud as a force for good in society.

Source: https://issuu.com/torontoartscape/docs/artscape_vision2017_final, 2019

to participate in the creative arts, as well as set out goals in driving forward a number of renewal and development issues. These bottom-up organisations emphasise participation and engagement in a number of diverse creative arts projects and community initiatives. The organisation focused on in the Canadian case study, Artscape, is one such organisation. Artscape has a wealth of literatures, detailing projects and also setting out priorities for the wider social issues affecting the community.

Concluding remarks

This chapter has examined the key debates in the scholarly literature and in practice, around the creative economy, creative arts and wider economic development. Moreover, it has highlighted the key gaps in these debates and the importance of recognising the role of both the creative arts and the creative economy in economic development initiatives. As the underpinning approach of the book – behavioural governance – argues, the importance of the success of the creative economy, arts and broader economic development is often grounded in policy-makers' abilities to change behaviour. The comparative focus of the book brings new knowledge to these established debates, by applying the behavioural approach across three comparative national case studies, and in investigating the role of the creative economy and creative arts in economic development initiatives. The three cases, as will be unpacked in the following chapter that addresses the conceptual debates in detail, also bring about differing institutional architectures that must be examined in the comparative behavioural context. The resultant debates around freedom, structure and agency through nudge are also key to the comparative focus of the book. The differing governance and institutional designs of the cases – and across the different creative arts and economic development initiatives in each case – also have the potential to affect the extent and success of nudge and behaviour-based policies. The following chapter unpacks in detail the philosophical approach of the book, the new knowledge that research brings to these established debates, and the methodological approach to the creative economy and economic development.

References

Akram, S. (2019) *Re-thinking contemporary political behaviour: The difference that agency makes* Abingdon: Routledge

Bailey, N. and Pill, M. (2015) Can the state empower communities through localism? An evaluation of recent approaches to neighbourhood governance in England *Environment and Planning C: Government and Policy* 33 (2): 289–304

Beebeejaun, Y., Durose, C., Rees, J., Richardson, J. and Richardson, L. (2015) Public harm or public value? Towards coproduction in research with communities *Environment and Planning C: Government and Policy* 33 (3): 552–565

Belfiore, E. (2018) Whose cultural value? Representation, power and creative industries *International Journal of Cultural Policy* 26 (3): 383–397

Bennett, T. (2018) 'Essential – passion for music': Affirming, critiquing, and practising passionate work in creative industries. In: Martin, L. and Wilson, N. (eds) *The Palgrave handbook of creativity at work* London: Palgrave Macmillan

Bilton, C. and Puttnam, L. (2007) *Management and creativity: From creative industries to creative management* Oxford: Wiley

Bowles, S. and Gintis, H. (2002) Social capital and community governance *The Economic Journal* 112: 419–436

Bull, A. and Jones, B. (2006) Governance and social capital in urban regeneration: A comparison between Bristol and Naples *Urban Studies* 43 (4): 767–786

Buller, J., Dönmez, P. E., Standring, A. and Wood, M. (2019) Depoliticisation, post-politics and the problem of change. In: Buller, J., Dönmez, P., Standring, A. and Wood, M. (eds) *Comparing strategies of (de)politicisation in Europe* London: Palgrave Macmillan

Castles, F. (1981) How does politics matter?: Structure or agency in the determination of public policy outcomes *European Journal of Political Research* 9 (2): 911–932

Cerny, P. (1990) *The changing architecture of politics: Structure, agency and the future of the state* London: Sage

Clements, J. (2018) Community resources for small city creativity? Rethinking creative economy narratives at the Blue Mountains Music Festival *Australian Geographer* 49 (4): 537–552

Comunian, R. (2011) Rethinking the creative city: The role of complexity, networks and interactions in the urban creative economy *Urban Studies* 48 (6): 1157–1179

Crogan, P. (2018) Indie dreams: Video games, creative economy, and the hyperindustrial epoch *Games and Culture* Published online 13 February 2018 doi. org/10.1177/1555412018756708

Cunningham, S. (2002) From cultural to creative industries: Theory, industry and policy implications *Media International Australia incorporating Culture and Policy* 102 (1): 54–65

Czarnitzki, D. and Fier, A. (2002) Do innovation subsidies crowd out private investment? Evidence from the German service sector *ZEW Discussion Papers* 02-04 http://hdl.handle.net/10419/24802

Department for Culture, Media and Sport (DCMS) (2018) *The creative industries sector deal* London: UK Government

Evans, G. (2009) Creative cities, creative spaces and urban policy *Urban Studies* 46 (5–6): 1003–1040

Fjoord, J. (2009) Strategies for creative industries: An international review *Creative Industries Journal* 1 (2): 91–113

Florida, R. (2004) *The rise of the creative class and how it's transforming work, leisure, community and everyday life* New York: Basic Books

Florida, R. (2006) The flight of the creative class: The new global competition for talent *Liberal Education* 92 (3): 22–29

Florida, R. (2010) *Who's your city?: How the creative economy is making where to live the most important decision of your life* Toronto: Vintage

Forde, S. (2019) *Movement as conflict transformation: Rethinking peace and conflict studies* London: Palgrave Macmillan

Friedman, G. and Starr, H. (2002) *Agency, structure and international politics: From ontology to empirical inquiry* Abingdon: Routledge

Friedman, M. (1989/2016) *The Adam Smith Address* The suicidal impulse of the business community. In: Crow, R. T. (ed) The *best of business economics* New York: Palgrave Macmillan

Galloway, S. and Dunlop, S. (2007) A critique of the definitions of cultural and creative industries in public policy *International Journal of Cultural Policy* 13 (1): 17–31

Garnham, N. (2005) From cultural to creative industries: An analysis of the implications of the 'creative industries' approach to arts and media policy making in the United Kingdom *International Journal of Cultural Policy* 11 (1): 15–29

Hartley, J. (2005) *Creative industries* Oxford: Blackwell

Hayek, F. (1945) *The road to serfdom* Oxford: Oxford University Press

Hesmondhalgh, D. and Pratt, A. (2005) Cultural industries and cultural policy *International Journal of Cultural Policy* 11 (1): 1–13

Houston, S. (2019) Extending Bourdieu for critical social work. In: Webb, S. (ed) *The Routledge handbook of critical social work* London and New York: Routledge

Howkins, J. (2002) *The creative economy: How people make money from ideas* London: Penguin

John, P. (2017) *How far to nudge? Assessing behavioural public policy* Cheltenham: Edward Elgar

John, P., Smith, G. and Stoker, G. (2009) Nudge nudge, think think: Two strategies for changing civic behaviour *Political Quarterly* 80 (3): 361–370

King, A. and Crewe, I. (2013) *The blunders of our governments* London: Oneworld Publications

Kunzmann, K. (2004) Culture, creativity and spatial planning *Town Planning Review* 75 (4): 383–404

Lombard, M. (2019) Informality as structure or agency? Exploring shed housing in the UK as informal practice *International Journal of Urban and Regional Research* Published online 29 January 2019 //doi.org/10.1111/1468-2427.12705

Malinowski, B. and Howkins, J. (2018) *Creative ecologies: Where thinking is a proper job* Abingdon: Routledge

Markusen, A. (2006) Urban development and the politics of a creative class: Evidence from a study of artists *Environment and Planning A* 46: 1139–1159

Markusen, A. and Wassall, G. (2008) Defining the creative economy: Industry and occupational approaches *Economic Development Quarterly* 22 (1): 24–45

McKee, K. (2015) Community anchor housing associations: Illuminating the contested nature of neoliberal governing practices at the local scale *Environment and Planning C: Government and Policy* 33 (5): 1076–1091

Miller, T. (2010) Cultural policy in *The encyclopedia of literary and cultural theory* Oxford: Wiley

Moe, T. (1989) The politics of bureaucratic structure In: Chubb, J. and Peterson, P. (eds) *Can the government govern?* Washington, DC: Brookings Institution

Nozick, R. (1974) *Anarchy, state and utopia* New York: Basic Books

O'Brien, D. (2013) *Cultural policy: Management, value and modernity in the creative industries* Abingdon: Routledge

Paquette, J. (2018) Creative economy and culture: Challenges, changes and futures of the creative industries *The Journal of Arts Management, Law, and Society* 48 (2): 148

Peterson, C. (2019) Exploring 'inspiration' and the library's potential role in the creative process *Arlis Art Libraries Society UK & Ireland Conference* 16 July 2019

Pleasants, N. (2019) Free will, determinism and the 'problem' of structure and agency in the social sciences *Philosophy of the Social Sciences* Published online 17 December 2018 doi.org/10.1177/0048393118814952

Ponzini, D. and Rossi, U. (2010) Becoming a creative city: The entrepreneurial mayor, network politics and the promise of an urban renaissance *Urban Studies* 47 (5): 1037–1057

Power, D. (2011) Priority sector report: Creative and cultural industries? Europa Innova paper no. 16.

Pratt, A. (2005) Cultural industries and public policy: An oxymoron? *International Journal of Cultural Policy* 11 (1): 31–44

Purdue, D. (2001) Neighbourhood governance: Leadership, trust and social capital *Urban Studies* 38 (12): 2211–2224

Radomska, J., Wołczek, P., Sołoducho-Pelc, L. and Silva, S. (2019) The impact of trust on the approach to management – a case study of creative industries *Sustainability* 11 (3): 816

Ren, H. (2018) The aesthetic scene: A critique of the creative economy in urban China *Journal of Urban Affairs Special Issue* Published online 22 March 2018 doi/abs/10.1080/07352166.2018.1443011

Robinson, F. Shaw, K. and Davidson, G. (2005) On the side of the angels: Community involvement in the governance of neighbourhood renewal *Local Economy* 6 (1): 61–73

Rodrigues, M. and Franco, M. (2019) Composite index to measure cities' creative performance: An empirical study in the Portuguese context *Sustainability* 11 (3): 774

Seyfang, G. and Haxeltine, A. (2012) Growing grassroots innovations: Exploring the role of community-based initiatives in governing sustainable energy transitions *Environment and Planning C: Government and Policy* 30 (3): 381–400

Silliman, S. (2001) Agency, practical politics and the archaeology of culture contact *Journal of Social Archaeology* 1 (2): 190–209

Spencer, H. (1982) [1873] *The man versus the state* New York: Liberty Fund

Suciu, M., Istudor, L., Spînu, D. and Năsulea, C. (2018) Cultural and creative economy: Challenges and opportunities for Romania. In: Mărginean, S., Ogrean, C. and Orăştean, R. (eds) *Emerging issues in the global economy* New York: Springer

Sullivan, H. (2001) Modernisation, democratisation and community governance *Local Government Studies* 27 (3): 1–24

Syamsudin, M. and Subono, N. (2018) Political opportunity structure and the success of Temanggung tobacco: Peasant resistance towards government regulation 81/1999 *International Journal of Social Sciences* 4 (2)

Taylor, M. (2007) Community participation in the real world: Opportunities and pitfalls in new governance spaces *Urban Studies* 44 (2): 297–317

Tepper, S. (2002) Creative assets and the changing economy *The Journal of Arts Management, Law, and Society* 32: 159–168

Volkerling, M. (2001) From cool Britannia to hot nation: Creative industries' policies in Europe, Canada and New Zealand *International Journal of Cultural Policy* 7 (3): 437–455

Waitt, G. and Gibson, C. (2009) Creative small cities: Rethinking the creative economy in place *Urban Studies* 46 (5): 1223–1246

Wendt, A. (1995) Constructing international politics *International Security* 20 (1): 71–81

Wiesand, A. and Soendermann, M. (2005) *The 'creative sector': An engine for diversity, growth, and jobs in Europe* European Cultural Foundation, 1 September

Winegar, J. (2006) *Creative reckonings: The politics of art and culture in contemporary Egypt* Stanford, CA: Stanford University Press

Wyszomirski, M. (2004) *Defining and developing creative sector initiatives* Ohio: Ohio University Press

3 Governance and institutional context
Policy, behaviour and communities

This chapter examines and applies the underpinning institutional and governance approaches to the debates outlined in the previous chapters. These debates focus on the types of governance enacted in the creative sector in the case-study areas, and the established institutional and governing contexts within the cases (inter alia, Sorensen, 2013, 2012, 2002; Bevir and Rhodes, 2008; Bevir and Rhodes, 2006; Bevir, 2005) in the creative sector and economic development initiatives. The chapter will examine theoretical positions (Panizza and Miorelli, 2013) that will then be examined in the following empirical case-study chapters. The institutional approach of the book focuses on governance processes within the cases, particularly in terms of the investment in the creative sector and in examining the ways these policies affect the goals of economic development and renewal. The governance and institutional approach draws upon the established conceptual ideas of behavioural public policy in terms of governance and institutional theory. The behavioural approach to public policy emphasises the key tensions and relations between key actors in the political economy of economic development programmes: who is funding; what is the relationship between specific projects in the case studies and the wider strategic aims of the funding programmes; where does power lie; where does cooperation occur; what are the short- and long-term effects of the policy goals and investment in the creative sector, politically and economically? These questions are focused on community engagement, job creation and funding levels as part of economic development and urban development initiatives in the empirical national case studies.

Why behaviourism?

Philosophically, this book focuses on the constructivist paradigm. More specifically, the research employs the behavioural approach: this is selected as there is a need to understand behaviours of actors in the creative economy, and in the different roles engaged in delivery of economic development initiatives and their governance. The key themes of debates identified in the previous chapter demonstrate the focus on differing levels of governance mechanisms; the historical importance of both EU structural funds and foreign direct investment (FDI) in supporting the creative economy and wider economic development; and the role of small and medium enterprises (SMEs) and third-sector organisations in driving innovation across the creative sector.

Comparative analysis and linkage to institutions

Federal and unitary systems

Of course, the focus on behaviour in public policy necessitates an examination of the other side of the conceptual coin: institutions. In unpacking the role of governance and institutions in this book, the creative sectors in the comparative cases are products of the institutional systems and governance processes in the respective nation states. The clear distinction between the cases is their federal and unitary devolved nature. Moreover, the federal nature of the German and Canadian cases involves the overlapping nature of governance decision-making. This takes place through the need for regional and national competencies. Moreover, there is the devolved nature of the UK, in terms of both the devolved nations but also the emergence of new regional governance in England with the advent of the city regions and combined authorities. These factors will also be examined in the context of funding and policy priorities across the cases. For example, will these established competencies provide a bigger role for regional and local delivery, or are national (and in some cases supranational) policies and funding streams more vital in the creative sector? These differences in the respective case-study governance institutions and architectures are examined in depth across each of the case-study areas, as these differing institutional mechanisms may have implications for the delivery of governance of the creative sector in the cases, and this in turn may affect policy goals, funding and the roles of communities. More recently, as Bulmer and Joseph (2016) argue, the roles of institutions are the products of contested mediations and bargaining over time that constrain or unlock processes between a set of actors. These institutional architectures, as the ongoing products of emerging interactions, can be malleable in changing membership or the rules of the game. However, these roles have been conceptualised as drivers for integration and bargaining across arenas. These contexts drive the priorities for funding and policy goals for the creative sector across the case-study areas. As noted in the previous chapter, there are two sides identifiable in the broader creative sector. This gives rise to institutional and governance questions around delivery and the roles of actors inside and outside institutional and governing arenas.

Rationality

The behavioural approach is also one that interrogates information – is the information supplied from governments to individuals in policy design perfect? Even if it were, it does not solve the problem for policy-makers that although individuals are provided with perfect information, they may disbelieve it. Though the choices of individuals are often shaped by nudge, the resultant debate of freedom and paternalism is conceptually difficult to resolve. The role of structure and agency in this debate is also one that the book can reframe by applying the problem to economic development initiatives. As will be discussed in more detail in the following chapter, the role of liberalism is a key problem for behaviourism. The role of nudges underpinning policy design in order to change behaviours has been one that has enjoyed measures of success in some policy arenas, and less in others. As John (2017) notes, the success of nudge policies lies in their subtleties.

The role of national, regional and local governance design in comparative behaviourism

Across several cases of the creative economy driving economic development initiatives – far more broadly than in the cases examined in this book – there are distinct influences on economic development priorities and the funding streams that support these projects. In terms of governance, this has tended to mean a focus on regional funding, through funds such as the Big Lottery Fund, Heritage Lottery Fund or dedicated funds such as Arts Council England, who in 2016 dedicated some £170 million to regions across England outside of London (The Guardian, 2016). The importance in regional difference is a key aspect in understanding the role of the creative economy in economic development, and in the governance that underpins these projects in design and delivery.

In terms of the comparative cases, the UK and other EU member states have benefitted from various structural funding programmes such as Horizon 2020, European Social Fund (ESF), European Regional Development Fund (ERDF) and the INTERREG programme. Across each of these funding streams there has been some focus on investment in the creative economy and creative arts more broadly. In terms of governance design, the role of local and regional levels means further complexities in governing economic development and the creative economy: chiefly, the navigation of these different levels for creative economy organisations and the contestations between actors around funds. For example, the UK Government, in 2018, set out plans for the UK Shared Prosperity Fund. This funding stream was aimed at replacing EU Structural Funds, but also raised more questions than it offered solutions.

Blurring lines and disrupting theory

Though this book takes a behavioural perspective, in order to compare across the cases the research takes into account the difference between institutional systems and governance mechanisms. The research in each case study focuses on funding, delivery and the roles of actors engaged in the creative economy, wider creative arts and their roles in driving economic development. The distinction between the formal and informal is vital: often, the roles of institutions and actors are formally distinct. The behavioural approach to public policy, however, moves this debate forward by disrupting established notions of structure and agency. The roles of actors engaged in the economic development initiatives through the creative economy may see these roles blurred: the problem of the wearing of too many hats, or the blurring of lines between formal and informal governance, for example. The structure–agency debate has extensively discussed the extent to which the agents become part of the structure, and the extent to which an institution may itself act as an agent. Furthermore, the roles of multiple institutions across differing levels of governance may lead to actors behaving as de facto institutions, through changing and uncertain conditions of the economy, central government funding and externalities such as economic crash, governance shifts such as devolution to city regions, or constitutional disruptions such as Brexit affecting the funding and policies they are constrained or enabled by. Differing levels of governance produce conditions where the institutional settings affect behaviours of actors in different ways: through funding, power relations, ideological difference, economic priorities or central mechanisms such as investment through FDI. These behaviours then produce the tensions between the actors that affect agency. The role of the creative economy in economic development may disrupt these established binaries of structure and agency: the actors engaged in the economic development initiatives may be nested in their localities or communities, and the effects on governance through institutional change and the behavioural consequences may include fragmentation, implications for accountability and disruptions to notions of legitimacy. These potential effects on governance delivery will be compared across the cases, drawing on the policy goals of national-level governments. Each of the case-study areas' goals for the creative economy as a driver for economic development will be examined, focusing on funding and delivery.

The problem of liberal paternalism

As Peter John (2017) argues, in his detailed examination of the role of liberal paternalism in nudge-based policy-making, it is the subtleties of nudge – its 'gentleness' (2017: 112) that reconciles the problem of structure and agency, and the related problem of nudge and freedom. The extent to which nudge can alter the behaviours of individuals is, as John notes (2017: 112), a complex relationship that falls across a cornucopia of moving policy spaces, around health, the environment and financial borrowing. Everyday policy nudges that have gone beyond the gentleness for which John argues – for example, the five-a-day healthy eating campaign or the 10,000 steps per day campaign – have become part of a wider discourse of national government policy in the media. So why should individuals react badly when it is for their ultimate benefit that policies are made? After all, how different is a government from a corporation? Yet individuals accept the nudges that marketing produces with quiet acquiescence – for after all, the products are sold. So why are social nudges so unique? Is it the perception of the reduction of liberty, the lack of trust in government from individuals or something more profound? In examining both rational and irrational behaviours, the question of liberal paternalism is one that is not just about nudge but also rather about belief. The extent of the nudge, as John argues, is vital; the temptation for liberals is to 'attack libertarian paternalism because even soft paternalism requires some constraint on autonomy' (John, 2017: 110). Indeed, as John notes elsewhere in his discussion of the ethics of nudge, the problem of assuming perfect information, informing rational choices, is often disrupted by rational solutions being offered through nudge to temper emotional irrational responses of individuals. We must also consider that there is a possibility that individuals will operate under the assumption (as will be covered at length later in this chapter in the discussion about trust and nudge) that all paternalistic information is imperfect and to be ignored or treated with suspicion. If we consider this to be, even at its least extent, a factor in how individuals treat nudge-based policy, there is the problem of public engagement with policy. As John argues, it is vital that successful and sustainable policies enjoy public support. The sense of perceived misinformation is perhaps not as profound as a limitation on individual freedom, but can be understood as criticism of individual choices, in areas around food consumption, health and the environment. However, the perceived limitations on individual freedoms are also, in the case of economic development, fair game for criticisms that attack the targeted nature of nudge:

> The argument is also that certain categories of people are subject to behaviour change interventions, which may not be true; and, in any case, certain categories of people, notably the poor, have always been on the receiving end of government policies and research efforts, such as those who are on the welfare. Nudge is no different in that respect. And a lot of nudges are applied to the whole population.
>
> (John, 2017: 114)

Of course, the tension between bottom-up movements and top-down economic development has been mitigated in some cases by the use of co-production or co-creation, but the barriers to achieving lasting economic development initiatives are captured by the problems of too heavy a nudge – as noted earlier, the physical changes to an area and the perception that changes are being done *to*, rather than *with*, communities and areas undergoing economic development initiatives. This kind of mistrust evidently makes efforts to nudge far more problematic. The issue of gentrification often both drives and results from housing-stock change, business development and other physical changes to landscape and community environment, such as infrastructure funded by FDI.

Governing economic development and the importance of behaviours and nudge: nudge as an ongoing exchange relationship

Perhaps the most consistent, and enduring, obstacle to achieving sustainable economic development lies in the role of behaviours and nudge, which can be viewed more broadly as an ongoing exchange relationship between institutions and agents. This is an important point, as the major barriers that face economic development projects are grounded in debates over structure and agency. Indeed, in some aspects, the idea of economic development can itself be seen as a kind of liberal paternalism. However, the issues that often frustrate economic development projects are rooted in misunderstandings of nudge. The perceived failure to consult or engage with communities over development, physical changes to areas and the changing demographic of developed areas – often through ideas of gentrification – have fuelled a mistrust in economic development and policy-makers driven by less-than-subtle nudges. The role of behaviour in economic development is key to achieving successful and sustainable change, though the complexities of such change are not just confined to physical change to town centres, or to housing stock. Moreover, in terms of engaging individuals and communities, economic development initiatives face challenges of how and when to engage, while minimising the risk of too large a nudge. The behavioural literature acknowledges this issue, particularly focused on the problem of engagement in the policy-making process. Using the thinking approach to policy as an alternative to nudge, and asking citizens to participate in the decision-making process to formulate policy, there are still obstacles in facilitating engagement:

> Most of the nudge policies worked in the sense of delivering changes in behaviour … but it was much harder to conclude that many of the think policies were as effective … the organisation found it hard to respond with activities for the citizens to participate in. The citizens were mobilised to turn from complainers into deliberators, but the infrastructure and support were not there to allow them to do so.
>
> (John, 2017: 126)

We might easily transpose this problem to the broad church of economic development. The vast policy challenges that often large-scale economic development or renewals initiatives take on encompass housing, business development, green space, community space, transport, education, healthcare, employability and community engagement. The potential for engagement here is vast, but obviously complex. The potential for mistrust in nudges brought about by economic development initiatives is also significant. This is driven by problems such as rapid change, top-down development and a lack of consultation among communities. Why should this broader problem be significant for the creative economy?

Creative economy: agents or structure?

Why should the creative economy be different in terms of behaviours and nudge, and why does this matter for economic development? The answer lies in two areas. The proposed UK Shared Prosperity Fund and the Renewal plan for cities, set out by Theresa May in 2018 and 2019, for example, is an attempt to replace EU Structural Funds in the UK regions. However, there is substantial risk of ideological clash between the regions and Westminster as to allocation and the priorities these funds are directed to. Equally, and more globally, there is a blurring of lines with structure and agency in terms of the creative economy: where organisations are bottom-up grassroots outfits, or SMEs, they interact with and are driven by communities and individuals, rather than reinforcing institutional structures. Agents in this way may eventually move towards becoming institutions themselves: they embark on an inevitable, irreversible direction of travel that sees them becoming part of existing institutional arrangements.

Behaviour, nudge and freedom

For liberals, the problem of nudge – as noted elsewhere in this chapter – lies in its paternalism. As with nudges experienced by individuals that come from the private sector, why should an individual not choose to spend all their income on the latest smartphone or tablet? Why should this nudge be different from the policy-based behaviour changes from government? The defence offered by some liberal commentators, echoing Mill's harm principle, is that individual agents should be free to make their own mistakes and choices.

Self-governance

In making sense of the disruption caused practically and conceptually by the rapid rise of creative arts organisations, we find more questions than answers. In making sense of the self-organisation of creative arts organisations, the book can disrupt several established concepts such as aspects of governance and institutional thought. Within these governance approaches, key aspects such as partnerships, structure and agency, and governance networks are disrupted and need to be reframed by the emergence of creative arts organisations. In bringing further new knowledge to the conceptual arena, we argue here that aspects of post-institutional thought, and governance concepts such as networks, are also disputed by the organisation, outside the institutional space, of creative arts organisations. In approaching this argument, we set out key propositions. First, we contend that the self-organisation of creative arts organisations – discussed in detail in the following sections – is not something we can conceptualise as a system of self-governance. Second, we further argue that the self-organisation of creative arts organisations is not a system of networks or collaborative governance, which challenges approaches such as network governance and the new public governance. Finally, the book argues that the importance of this self-organisation is an emerging system driven by rapid agency-based changes and constantly evolving technologies, rather than a form of self-'governance', as this language is fundamentally disrupted by the self-organisation of creative arts organisations, operating as they do outside any established institutional arena. Therefore, while it is a system of self-organisation, it is not one the book can describe as self-governance. It is precisely this disruption to established understandings of the notion of self-governance that brings new conceptual knowledge to these debates.

The organisation of creative arts organisations poses a disruptive problem for theory. How do we conceptualise a new order, outside established institutional walls and norms, outside established regulatory principles? The first way of approaching this imposing question is to focus on the nature of the self- organisation of creative arts organisations. We contend that these interactions, driven by code or by digital exchange, lie outside the formal and informal processes of accepted norms of governance and institutions.

The self-organisation of creative arts organisations poses several questions to established conceptual approaches and practical institutional processes. Here the book addresses the accepted ideas of self-governance and disrupts these with new knowledge: the self-organisation of creative arts organisations. We then move on to discuss how post-institutional thinking, more broadly conceived, cannot account for the types of exchanges and interactions we see in the self-organisation of creative arts organisations. Furthermore, we address existing debates within governance theory that emphasise self-organisation, such as the role of governance networks. Such governance designs have regularly been posited as self-organising (Borzel, 1998, 2011), but have in reality tended to be driven by power relations that are the product of one or more competing institutional actors within the particular policy space. Moreover, we argue, such formal or informal governance arrangements are typically mediated through institutional levers or processes. These governance arrangements also take place amid a potential backdrop of collaborative tension. Confusion around communication, leadership, resources and power relations all frustrate the network process. The book suggests, therefore, that none of the established conceptual governance approaches are able to make sense of the organisation of creative arts organisations. Rather, the book argues that the self-organisation of creative arts organisations acts as a major disruption to established and accepted notions of governance and institutional theory.

Do creative arts organisations disrupt ideas of governance?

The notion of self-government is most closely associated with Foucault's (2019, 1980) work on self and institutions. In disrupting this theoretical approach, we argue that the prism of self-government does not account for the behaviours of agents engaged in creative arts organisations, being, as it is, focused on the role of the reactions of individuals to institutional and post-institutional systems. However, the book does argue that the prism of self-governance explains the behaviours of both creative arts' self-organising systems and the individual agents who compose these. Elsewhere, the book has argued these systems do not compose institutional arrangements. Their existence is driven by the exchange of assets among agents, outside the established formal regulatory institutional structures and mechanisms. In disrupting the notion of self-governance, the book argues that this framework needs to be redrawn in order to understand the exchange, self-organisation and workings within creative arts organisations.

The original notion of self-governance evolved from Foucault's writings on risk, self, madness and health. The notion of self-governance is also predicated on an individual reaction to mediation through institutions and rules, notably the idea of observation (Foucault, 2019). Self-governance in this vein is a product of institutional life and seeks to assert a new politics, whether driven by the creation of a new radical politics or through the idea of self, biopolitics. This approach has clear key differences to the self-organisation of creative arts organisations, which are also, though in a different vein, a reaction to and a product of institutional norms and life. They are individual agents connecting through a virtual institutional world, which is not joined through any of these edifices of the established notion of self-governance. These edifices, such as morality, risk and health, are not apparent in the self-organisation of creative arts organisations. Rather these are coded, agent-based interactions that operate outside of any established institutional arena. They are not guided by ideas of moralities or notions of self-governance but rather by coding and ideas of interactions between agents, dealing with moral or critical action problems on an ad hoc basis. As noted earlier, they are not a reaction to institutions that leads to a new set of politics, a lobby or a cause *within* established institutional norms. Rather, the self-organisation of creative arts organisations (while, as we have noted elsewhere, it is a reaction to and a product of institutional life) operates outside of the institutional arena. The book cannot make sense of this emergence and self-organisation through established, accepted ideas, nor through the post-institutional prism. Instead, the book argues that the self-organisation of creative arts organisations practically and conceptually disrupts accepted notions of self-governance to such an extent that the book cannot express the self-organisation of creative arts organisations in a way that scholars would recognise as 'governance'.

Existing debates around the idea of self-governance are driven by the underpinning idea of ethics and subjectivity that continues to be refracted through varying scales and levels of ongoing existing institutional life (Luxon, 2008; Fraser, 2003; Petersen, 1997). This is also a key divergence from the self-organisation of creative arts organisations. In the Foucauldian notion of self-governance, the subject is still operated on and through via law-making bodies and established structures. They are self-governing only to the extent that this may be a coping mechanism or reaction against such accepted norms, but they essentially remain as subjects and objects within the established structured mediating rules of the game. This is markedly different from the self-organisation of creative arts organisations. While they, like the notion of self-governance to an extent, have emerged as a reaction to and a product of these establishment structures, they are not subjects or objects in any sense, and this is what makes the understanding of their self-organisation so vital.

These key differences from the Foucauldian notion of self-governance are also a product, evidently, of rapidly evolving technological digital platforms across which interactions are conducted. The emergence of self-governance as a *response* construct to the mediations and operation of institutional life is played out in the areas of discourses of health, esteem and, more latterly, against the canvas of a globalised political economy (Hay, 2006; Fraser, 2003).

This is within the confines of a life in which 'individuals are faced with the paradoxical task of living against themselves and experiencing their lives in certain important ways as being "impossible"' (Luxon, 2008: 377). As Luxon goes on to argue, the crux of self-governance for Foucault, and the importance of its meaning in individuals' lives, is driven by the need to 'overcom[e] these divisions' (Luxon, 2008: 378). The role of self-governance is vital in enabling the individual to exist apart from societal binding arrangements and norms, while living an ethical life. The ability of the individual to exercise this role, however, is, for Foucault, constrained by horizons and imagination. As Luxon (2008: 378), goes on to suggest, in Foucault's terms, individuals are unable to avoid being affected by the conditions of institutions as they cannot help but:

> unwittingly replicate the very structures that are the conditions and limits to their claims to self-hood, the others have since tempered the productive coherence of disciplinary techniques and their contribution to radical politics ... the seeming inability of individuals to discover and assert normative principles by which to act.

However, as noted earlier, the critical question here is why the individual seeks to actualise a system of self-governance. This seems to be a step for Foucault in reform, through a radical politics, or a coping mechanism to enable the individual to exist as if outside these institutional constraints, when all the time living within them. The differences here are key. While some may argue the self-organisation of creative arts groups represents a form of self-governance, there are marked differences in both form and purpose. In the first instance, the self-organisation of creative arts organisations is not what the book might constitute as governance: it does not engage with regulatory norms, and is not part of an institutional structure. Indeed, the purpose of self-organisation of creative arts organisations is not to reform or radicalise existing established institutional structures; rather, it is to actually, not *subconsciously*, exist and operate outside of these structures. Although, as Luxon (2008: 384) goes on to argue, Foucault's notion of ethical self-governance comprises: 'relations, their links, their imbrication with those other things, which are the wealth, resources, means of subsistence, the territory with its specific qualities'.

Moreover, in achieving and actualising the notion of self-governance, Foucault is highly prescriptive. Set against the self-organisation of creative arts organisations, this is a vast difference, leading us to reframe the notion of the idea of self-governance. Here we have a set of individual agents who are connected through digital and technological means, who may not know each other outside this exchange of assets. The role of fear is also an important consideration in Foucault's notion of self-governance. In achieving self-governance, individuals feel they have become 'no longer dependent on the terms and authority structures of external order' (Luxon, 2008: 391). The book asserts this is not self-governance in real terms, but instead, imagined self-governance. The self-organisation of creative arts organisations disrupts the notion of self-governance. At first glance, it may seem to share some of the aspects Foucault prioritises around the notion: organisation, agency and self-control. In the institutional arena, however, the fundamental and key differences are that, first, the self-organisation of creative arts organisations is not a type of governance; and second, and equally importantly, the established idea of self-governance is that it is an individual reaction to a set of institutional conditions that the individual is reacting against, while existing within these actual structures. In other words, the goal of self-governance is to reform the institutional arena and the conditions for the individual within those structures. The self-organisation of creative arts organisations disrupts this idea. It is not an attempt to subconsciously challenge or disrupt the existing institutional arrangements from within these structures. Instead, the entire self-organisation process of creative arts organisations is in its entirety a disruption to institutional and regulatory orders, taking place *outside* these institutional structures.

With this in mind, the conceptual importance of this self-organisation as new knowledge also leads us to examine how the self-organisation of creative arts organisations therefore challenges accepted notions of institutional discourse approaches. Though theoretical lenses like post-structural discourse theory accept the idea that institutions are evolving, incomplete structures (Panizza and Miorelli, 2013) and that these are unable to fully capture the actions of agents (Glynos and Howarth, 2007: 139, cited in Panizza and Miorelli, 2013: 309). For institutional thinkers, the logic then follows that the institutional settings must rebalance and adjust to draw in agents that lie outside of their arenas. This approach, however, demonstrates just how vast is the challenge the self-organisation of creative arts organisations presents to established institutional settings. The ideas of self-governance and post-structural discursive ideas of how discourse operates on agents through these settings are both predicated on the notion that eventually institutions will evolve to include these agents. However, an acceptance of an institutional environment where time is driven by shifts driven by crisis leads to an institutional context of path dependence (Hay, 2001: 203, cited in Panizza and Miorelli, 2013: 309):

> Time within this [institutional] framework is textured and contoured, alternating (though in no preordained or predetermined manner) between decisive, intense and contested moments of crisis and paradigm shift on the one hand, and longer, slower, more drawn out periods of iterative change and path dependent institutional evolution on the other.

This institutional environment, for institutionalism thinkers, is one where agents may seek to disrupt or challenge established processes. The means of institutions correcting themselves or recovering may vary, across time or through policy change, but will eventually occur. Often, these are modes of change that institutionalise reactions of agents or campaigns for change. The notion of self-governance, as Foucault sets out, is a reaction to this and the related institutional discourses that operate on and through the individual agent. None of these approaches, however, can make sense of the self-organisation of creative arts organisations and the way they operate outside these established arenas.

Self-organising networks

The established model of governance delivery over the last 20 years in terms of collaboration has been, across varying national, regional and local delivery systems, one of networks or partnerships, composed of various public, private and third-sector actors across multi-levels. These systems have been conceptualised in scholarly debate as network governance (Kjaer, 2011), partnership governance (Borzel, 1998) or multi-agency working, and have led to approaches characterising the role of collaboration between the third sector and local government as the new public governance (Osborne, 20010, 2006). There is, in each of these approaches, a strong emphasis – and causal claims by scholars – on the role of self-organisation. This book contends, however, that this idea is fundamentally different to the self-organisation of creative arts organisations. The decisions taken across governance networks or partnerships are nested in existing institutional systems (Panizza and Miorelli, 2013), such as funding decisions by central government; ideological change driven centrally by political parties; funding conditions from supranational organisations; and are mediated through national government institutional compliance with global governance agreements.

The effect of complexities in self-organised governance networks is also a behavioural problem: role interpretation in governance is further illustrated by the role of multi-agency working. Drawing on multi-agency delivery and collaborative exchanges that underpin network governance, there are examples of role interpretation that constrained the effectiveness of policy delivery and the joined-up nature of the multi-agency system. These issues were alongside other obstacles caused by role interpretation, such as a lack of communication, clarity and stress. Further issues created by the problem of role interpretation were those of lack of coherence and trust between the actors in the multi-agency setting.

Additionally, the role of multi-agency and network or partnership delivery in governance settings has grown rapidly in the last 20 years, giving rise to changes in role perception of officials and actors. An example of this is given in research by Sorensen (2006) as she examines the role of Danish municipal politicians who, like many holders of political office, are embedded in working with multi-agency networks. Sorensen argues that the role of these officials has shifted from politicians to metagovernors, enmeshed in and overseeing a complex network of decision-making, power and delivery, as 'no single actor is capable of governing society. Governance today is a complex and interactive process' (Sorensen, 2006: 107). The role of networks and partnerships in governance increases the number of actors in governance and the tendency for different interpretations to affect outcomes in policy. The weight of these ideas and these consequences for delivery emphasise the importance of interpretation of the different actors in governance.

Informal governance

Notions of informal governance (Ayres, 2017) have tended to come about as a product of long-standing relationships at varying levels of formal governance mechanisms. Over time, these relationships and exchanges become nested: they are driven by long-established mutual trust and personal contacts. These ideas of informal governance, however, are not an answer in conceptually making sense of the self-organisation of creative arts organisations, for two main reasons. First, the informal nature of governance may reflect interactions and exchanges, but these take place within the formal nature of governance structures. Second, these are driven by personal connections, rather than the technological-driven agent-based exchange and interaction we see in the self-organisation of creative arts organisations.

In this chapter, we have argued that the notion of self-governance, most often associated with Foucault, can be reframed by the self-organisation of creative arts organisations. As creative arts organisations operate outside established regulatory structures and institutional mechanisms, we argue that the organisation of creative arts is one of self-governance. Conceptually, this is important because the rapid rise and evolution of creative arts frustrates regulation and institutionalisation. This enables us to reframe the Foucauldian approach, which is centred on the individual and the underpinning idea of biopolitics. Do creative arts organisations allow us to reframe this idea of self-governance, as creative arts organisations often exist outside traditional governance arrangements and the institutional context, and distinct from governance partnership arrangements?

These interactions represent a far different aspect of organisation, as they involve multiple actors, rather than merely the self. The language here is also important, as is the use of code in the self-organisation of creative arts organisations. The term 'governance' is one that is not adequate to sufficiently capture the self-organisation of creative arts organisations. While the book can, as we have argued previously, see creative arts organisations as a reaction and a consequence of institutional constraints, it cannot see them as part of a post-institutional framework. We argue instead that the self-organising nature of creative arts organisations enables us to disrupt the notion of self-governance, moving the conceptual debate onwards from the underpinning idea of biopolitics to an emerging arena that is beyond spatial, beyond established notions of governance and related language, and even potentially beyond the established idea of the agent.

Mistrust, disengagement and austerity are all potential barriers to change in driving a creative sector and in using this to foster economic development. Likewise, there may be established modes of practice, rituals and inherited thinking (tradition) across the cases that impede participation and engagement in the creative sector.

Moreover, there is the potential for mistrust, driven by assumptions on the quality of evidence bases around the need for behaviour change (such as perfect versus imperfect information, and mistrust of elites). The complexities of existing governance models have perhaps tended to frustrate community engagement, widening the distance between decision-makers and those they represent.

The perceived failure to consult or engage with communities over development, physical changes to areas or job creation in differing sectors is a potential risk in the case studies. The case-study chapters will focus on the role of institutions, governance and behaviour to interrogate the creative sector and its role in economic development in comparative contexts. Moreover, in terms of engaging individuals and communities, the creative sector and related renewal initiatives face challenges of how and when to engage with communities, and of top-down nudges failing to engage communities with the creative arts sector. The potential for mistrust in nudges brought about by economic development initiatives is also significant. This is driven by problems such as rapid change, top-down development and a lack of consultation among communities.

Comparative approach

The research focuses on three case studies with differing institutional and governance structures. In comparing across these systems, the book examines the institutional structure and mode of governance delivery. The German and Canadian systems are both federal in nature, with devolved (and in some instances, overlapping) competencies at regional or local levels. The UK case study is couched in the context of a unitary devolved state with a movement towards regional decentralisation in England. In comparing across these systems, the book will examine potential benefits and constraints that result from modes of governance that affect the creative sector and its role in driving economic development. In capturing the roles of non-state actors in the creative sector, the research examines the institutional structures and the agents that operate alongside, but outwith, these established structures. This methodological rationale is set out in depth in the following sections.

Methodological design

The research is driven by a constructivist paradigm of inquiry. This is to underpin the importance of the key governance and institutional questions that are posed in the research. The three case-study chapters are examined through the analysis of national-level policy strategies, policy goals and levels of spend and investment across the creative sector. Through studying established conceptual approaches of governance, the book will interrogate the governance, institutional roles and behaviours of the creative sector and will question the potential role of the creative sector in economic development across the three cases in the book. The empirical cases that follow this chapter will then focus on the roles of governance, institutions and behaviour. This approach focuses on potential disruptions to established thinking, and provides new knowledge in the fields of economic development and renewal. The approach moves forward work that emphasises participatory roles of culture and the arts in regeneration, such as that of Omar *et al.* (2016), Oakley and O'Connor (2015) and Romein *et al.* (2013). The focus on the creative sector and the arts more broadly also draws existing debates (Thaler, 2018; Sunstein, 2016) into a new policy arena.

Structure, agency, governance and behaviour

Philosophically the book begins from a constructivist position, embracing a reflexive hermeneutical idea that includes 'involvement with data in terms of … interpretation of materials through producing meanings, critique of interpretation of through theoretical perspectives such as power, politics and ideological positions … The ideal situation incorporates theory being re-moulded by the data' (Howell, 2013: 187). This approach emphasises a reality based on local shared constructions and experiences ontologically. As the methodology progresses through the book, epistemologically the findings will be discovered through the investigation (Howell, 2013: 29).

Conceptually, the book revisits established notions of governance and the structure–agency debate and examines the effects on institutional norms and policy-making that have arisen as a result of the effects of gentrification and legacy in the cases. The method employed within this approach begins by examining spending on the creative sector in large-scale economic development initiatives in the UK, Germany and Canada. Following this stage, the focus on the cases looks at policy strategies and the level of spend, who is funding, the time period of the project and the key actors engaged in delivery. There then follows a comparative contextual analysis of the policy strategies across these cases. This is then applied to the conceptual governance discussion in the book, focused on the implications for established governance and institutional debates. Using an interpretivist approach, the book draws upon the analysis of the policy strategy, funding and actors in delivery. Following this stage, the creative sector in the three case-study areas is then examined as a part of large-scale economic development programmes in the UK, Germany and Canada that have been constructed around creative economy and investment and development of this arena. The third stage of the methodology then moves on to critically examine the governance processes involved in the two case study chapters. Finally, the book revisits the established governance theory to examine the conceptual meanings of the analysis in the light of the

Table 3.1 Philosophical and methodological approach

Ontology	Epistemology	Methodological approach
Reality locally constructed, though shared by many	Linkage between the researcher and subject. Acceptance of subjectivity	Consensus built by many constructions including researcher's

Source: adapted from Howell, 2013: 29.

empirics captured across the case-study chapters. The theoretical perspectives of governance are revisited in light of the empirics set out in each of the case-study chapters.

Ontologically, the relationship between researcher and subject is driven by an acceptance of the shared constructions that have shaped the realities of the case studies. In this way, the researcher accepts the shared constructions of the case studies, as they are products of the differing political and economic contexts in each environment. Epistemologically, this gives rise to a separation between the researcher and subject, but an acceptance that reality is blurred between the two.

Table 3.1 below sets out the key philosophical and methodological approaches of the book, while also providing a framework for comparison across institutional differences. The three case studies are enacted within a devolved and decentralised unitary case (UK), and two federal case studies (Germany and Canada). The institutional context is vital in understanding the similarities and differences across the cases.

Key research question

What are the key organisations that drive the creative sector and what are the implications for economic development and governance?

Ancillary research questions

1   What is the role of creative arts organisations in economic development?
2   What are the key policy priorities for the creative sector?
3   What is the role of community participation and engagement in this process?
4   Does this take place in a formal or informal manner?

Concluding remarks

This chapter has examined the importance of the roles of institutions, agents and modes of governance in the creative sector and economic development.

The key issues of institutional theory, especially focused on debates around structure and agency, are set out here. The focus on the creative sector – as we have seen in Chapter 2 – has centred on the creative sector as an area of growth driven by central government investment and innovation; and also the more community-facing and bottom-up arts organisations. While each of these aspects of the debate are able to drive economic development, these underpinning tensions of governance and institutions are vital in explaining and making sense of the ways in which this takes place. This chapter has focused on the roles of behaviour in public policy, which will be used to unpack the role of governance processes, community engagement and participation in the creative sector in the following case-study chapters. Institutionalism will be used to investigate the role of investment and structures in the governance of the creative sector and to unpack the role of the creative sector in economic development across the cases. The opportunities and investments in the creative sector driven by government funding are examined, as are the constraints on the creative arts and the roles of bottom-up creative arts organisations. The book now turns to the first of the three case studies, the UK, focusing on the role of investment in and policy around the creative sector, and then moves on to focus on the roles of a bottom-up creative arts organisation, and the implications for economic development and governance.

References

Ayres, S. (2017) Assessing the impact of informal governance on political innovation *Public Management Review*, 19 (1): 90–107

Bevir, M. (2005) *New labour: A critique* Abingdon: Routledge

Bevir, M. and Rhodes, R. A. W. (2006) The life, death and resurrection of British governance *Australian Journal of Public Administration*, 65 (2): 59–69

Bevir, M. and Rhodes, R. (2008) The differentiated polity as narrative *The British Journal of Politics and International Relations* 10 (4): 729–734

Borzel, T. (1998) Organising Babylon: On the different conceptions of policy networks *Public Administration* 76 (2): 253–273

Borzel, T. (2011) Networks: Reified metaphor or governance panacea? *Public Administration* 89 (1): 49–63

Bulmer, S. and Joseph, J. (2016) European integration in crisis? Of supranational integration, hegemonic projects and domestic politics *European Journal of International Relations* 22 (4): 725–748

Foucault, M. (1980) *Power/knowledge: Selected interviews and other writings, 1972–1977* London: Pantheon

Foucault, M. (2019) *Ethics: Subjectivity and truth: Essential works of Michel Foucault 1954–1984* London: Penguin

Fraser, N. (2003) Rethinking recognition: Overcoming displacement and reification in cultural politics. In Hobson, B. (ed.) *Recognition struggles and social movements: Contested identities, agency and power* Cambridge: Cambridge University Press

Hay, C. (2006) Constructivist institutionalism. In: Binder, S., Rhodes, R. and Rockman, B. (eds) *The Oxford handbook of political institutions* Oxford: Oxford University Press

Howell, K. E. (2013) *An introduction to the philosophy of methodology* London: Sage

John, P. (2017) *How far to nudge? Assessing behavioural public policy* Cheltenham: Edward Elgar

Kjaer, A. (2011) Rhodes' contribution to governance theory: Praise, criticism and the future governance debate *Public Administration* 89 (1): 101–113

Luxon, N. (2008) Ethics and subjectivity practices of self-governance in the late lectures of Michel Foucault *Political Theory* 36 (3): 377–402

Oakley, K. and O'Connor, J. (eds) (2015) *The Routledge companion to the cultural industries* Abingdon: Routledge

Omar, S., Sakip, S. and Akhir, N. (2016) Bringing the new to the old: Urban regeneration through public arts *Procedia – Social and Behavioral Sciences* 234: 515–524

Osborne, S. (2006) The new public governance? *Public Management Review* 8 (3): 377–387

Osborne, S. (2010) *The new public governance: Emerging perspectives on the theory and practice of public governance* Abingdon: Routledge

Panizza, F. and Miorelli, R. (2013) Taking discourse seriously: Discursive institutionalism and post-structuralist discourse theory *Political Studies* 61 (2): 301–318

Petersen, A. (1997) Risk, governance and the new public health. In Petersen, A. and Bunton, R. (eds) *Foucault, health and medicine* Abingdon: Routledge

Romein, A, Nijkamp, J. E. and Trip, J. (2013) *Creativity-led regeneration: Towards an evaluation framework*. Presented at the AESOP-ACSP Joint Congress. Retrieved from http://hdl.handle.net/1765/94916

Schmidt, V. (2001) Federalism and state governance in the EU and the U.S.: An institutional perspective. In: Nicolaides, K. and Howse, R. (eds) *The Federal Vision* Oxford: Oxford University Press

Sorensen, E. (2002) Democratic theory and network *Governance Administrative Theory & Praxis* 24 (4): 693–720

Sorensen, E. (2006) Metagovernance: The changing role of politicians in processes of democratic governance *American Review of Public Administration* 36 (1): 98–114

Sorensen, E. (2012) Governance networks as a frame for inter-demoi participation and deliberation *Administrative Theory & Praxis* 34 (4): 509–532

Sorensen, E. (2013) Institutionalizing interactive governance for democracy *Critical Policy Studies* 7 (1): 72–86

Sorensen, E. (2014) The metagovernance of public innovation in governance networks *Policy & Politics* conference in Bristol, 16–17 September 2014

Sunstein, C (2016) *Why nudge?: The politics of libertarian paternalism* New Haven, CT: Yale University Press

Thaler, R. (2018) Nudge, not sludge *Nature*, 361(6401): 431–432

The Guardian (2016) Arts Council England celebrates the regions www.theguardian.com/culture/2016/jan/01/arts-council-england-celebrates-the-regions

4 UK

Take A Part

This first empirical case-study chapter examines the role of Take A Part (TAP) in Plymouth, in the south-west of England. This study investigates the role of creative arts in regeneration and community participation in urban renewal projects. This chapter investigates the UK governance and institutional contexts nationally in terms of policy-making, focused on the UK's Industrial Strategy for the creative sector. The chapter then moves on to unpack the role of a creative arts organisation and to address the conceptual and practical policy opportunities and challenges these examples present. Specifically, the chapter focuses on the role of the organisation in its method of working with communities outside established structures, and revisits structure and agency and institutional thought to ponder disruptions to existing ideas. Practically, the chapter critically analyses funding, partnerships and the ways in which the community has engaged with the creative arts through projects that target youth, health or social engagement in relation to debates regarding sustainability, education and urban renewal.

Governance and institutional context in the UK

This chapter begins by examining the governance and institutional context for the creative arts and the creative economy in UK central government policy-making. It then moves on to focus on the investment and funding through industrial strategy, before moving on to critically discuss the case study of Take A Part in Plymouth. In so doing, the chapter unpacks: the core aims of the book empirically, in unpacking the tensions between the creative economy and bottom-up creative arts movements; the importance of both of these sectors as drivers for economic development and renewal; and the national–regional comparisons derived from these empirics, policy histories and policy goals. The chapter then moves on to revisit the conceptual importance of these findings and debates. As noted in Chapters 2 and 3, there are tensions in making sense of the creative economy and creative arts sector (and not just in the UK). This chapter focuses on the UK Government's strategy for investing in the creative sector and then

Table 4.1 Political economy of the creative sector in the UK

Project	Funders	Level of governance	Key partners	Political era
Creative Industries Sector Deal	EU Structural Funds; UK Government Funds	Supranational; national; regional and devolved administrations	UK Government; regional and devolved administrations; EU; SMEs; HEIs	2015–
Creative Industries Strategy	EU Structural Funds; UK Government Funds; National Lottery	Supra national; national; local	UK Government; EU; third sector	2010–2015
Creative Industries Policy	EU Structural Funds; UK Government Funds	Supra national; national; local	UK Government; EU; Regional Development Agencies; local; private sector	1997–2010

moves on to examine the bottom-up roles of creative arts organisations in economic development.

The initial sections focus on national level policy goals of the UK's Industrial Strategy and then, subsequently, the direction of funding to support these ambitions. The context of the UK's Industrial Strategy, evidently, needs to be placed within the governance and institutional context. In terms of this context, there are moving policy spaces that may affect the prioritisation and funding of the creative arts and creative economy: namely, the process of the UK's exit from the European Union and the complexities around this process; the still-emerging patterns of regional and combined governance across England; and the role of funding for the creative arts and creative economy in the devolved nations. Furthermore, the post-Brexit landscape also demonstrates the need for the UK to invest in areas of strength, and also to support and bolster those regions where there is underinvestment, or large areas of inequality, unemployment and differential outcomes in terms of life chances and life expectancy. However, there is a problem in terms of participation, in that the investment in the creative arts has been somewhat asymmetric, favouring London and the South East. This disparity prompted investment in the regions, such as the £170 million that Arts Council England (ACE) distributed in 2017. The creative sector in the UK is characterised broadly, encompassing the following areas:

- Advertising and marketing
- Architecture
- Crafts
- Design: product, graphic and fashion design
- Film, TV, video, radio and photography
- Publishing
- Broad range of creative activities:
  - Digital media and ICT
  - Gaming industry
  - Art galleries, heritage and museums
  - Performing arts
                    (Department for Culture, Media and Sport (DCMS), 2018)

The focus on the creative economy in the UK Government's Industrial Strategy undoubtedly will need to balance investment in areas in need of renewal and economic development with those that are already flourishing. The role of the creative economy in driving economic development – through musical or cultural events, overlapping digital economy start-ups that create jobs, or through engagement and participation from communities – is a vital area of focus. The Industrial Strategy focuses on core themes of investment, job creation and employability: as can be seen in Box 4.1, the core principles refer to job creation and skills training; utilising the established overlap with digital technologies in the creative industries; and partnerships with universities as well as the development of small businesses across the creative sector. Each of these drivers for economic development is also part of an established business, educational or commercial institution. The conceptual importance of this will be examined in depth later on in this chapter, but it is worth noting that there is a great wealth of the creative arts sector that drives community engagement and participation through informal mechanisms, through bottom-up groups that sit outside the governance and institutional norms and mechanisms. The linkage between these two groups in achieving enduring economic development through the creative arts and the wider creative economy has proven problematic. This tension demonstrates the gap between investment and bottom-up projects in the creative arts. To be sure, both of these are potential drivers for economic development, but the gap between top-down investment in targeted areas and bottom-up creative sector groups is potentially problematic in terms of community engagement. Top-down investment may neglect areas of much-needed attention and development through the creative sector. The need for investment in the creative economy, however, forms a core part of industrial strategy in the UK. Box 4.1 shows the key focuses of the Creative Industries Sector Deal.

Box 4.1 Creative sector in UK industrial strategy

Industrial Strategy Creative Industries Sector Deal key sector deal policies at a glance

Places

Support creative centre across the country, to enable clusters of world-class businesses to increase GVA and employment. We will commit £20m over the next two years to roll out a Cultural Development Fund so that local partnerships can bid for investments in culture and creative industries, with industry contributing funding, networks and leadership.

Ideas

Open up Research and Development (R&D) funding to catalyse innovation. The Industrial Strategy Challenge Fund and industry will invest an estimated £58m to harness the power of immersive technologies and double the UK's share of the global creative immersive content market by 2025. We will also jointly invest £64m in an Arts and Humanities Research Council programme to deliver eight partnerships between universities and creative businesses across the UK, creating 900 business-led collaborations, 360 jobs and 65 new businesses, backed by a national Policy and Evidence Centre.

Business environment

Tackle copyright infringement, continue to address the transfer of value from creative industries and progress work on closing the value gap at the European and domestic levels. We will convene online intermediaries and rights holders to consider the need for and agree new Codes of Practice in: social media, digital advertising and online marketplaces. We will also extend investment for the successful 'Get it Right' copyright education campaign.

Reduce barriers to accessing finance for growth

The British Business Bank will seek to improve access to finance for high-growth firms outside London – including creative businesses – via a commercial investment programme to support clusters of business angels. We will help creative firms access finance by investing up to £4m (subject to business case) in a programme of intensive business investment readiness support.

Build on strong export performance to drive a Global Britain

We will create an industry and government Trade and Investment Board targeting a 50 per cent increase in creative industries exports by 2023.

People

To increase the supply and diversity of skills and talent in the creative industries, government will make up to £2m available (subject to business case) to support an industry-led creative careers programme aiming to reach at least 2,000 schools and 600,000 pupils in two years and industry development of apprenticeship standards. Industry will provide further leadership on diversity and scope expanding the voluntary Skills Investment Fund supporting on-the-job training.

Source: www.gov.uk/government/publications/creative-industries-
sector-deal/creative-industries-sector-deal-html

Box 4.2 Investment in the creative sector in the UK

In 2012, building on its work as a screen agency, the Yorkshire Content Fund was set up with backing from the European Regional Development Fund (ERDF), which has subsequently provided financial support to over 40 film and TV projects including *National Treasure, Dad's Army, '71* and *Peaky Blinders*. The region has seen strong growth with employment in the film and television industries increasing 88 per cent between 2009 and 2015, and turnover increasing by 247 per cent over the same period.

In Dundee, an early nucleus of creative businesses that generate games IP, targeted funding and responsive higher education institutions have supported the area to develop as one of the UK's most significant video-games development clusters, with more than 40 established games firms and 350 employees. Run from the same city, the UK Games Fund helps SMEs across the UK create new games IP. It now supports a community of around 100 UK video-games developers.

HBO's decision to film *Game of Thrones* in Belfast in 2010 has delivered spillover effects for the local creative economy, supporting a cluster of businesses including post-production house Yellowmoon and Belfast facilities company, Acorn Film and Video, who produce the Behind the Scenes packages for the show's website.

By introducing Local Industrial Strategies and further strengthening local leadership through Local Enterprise Partnerships and Mayoral Combined Authorities we will provide incentives to make a wider range of places attractive environments for creative businesses.

We have committed to investing £21m in Tech City UK over four years to expand into Tech Nation supporting digital companies and start-ups all across the UK, which will include many creative businesses. Regional hubs will be located in Cambridge, Bristol and Bath, Manchester, Newcastle, Leeds, Sheffield, Reading, Birmingham, Edinburgh, Glasgow, Belfast and Cardiff.

We have set out plans to strengthen infrastructure including funding from the National Productivity Investment Fund to grow Local Full Fibre Networks and further investment into the 5G Testbeds and Trials programme. This will allow creative businesses with a digital footprint to thrive anywhere in the UK by closing down digital coldspots.

On top of these cross-cutting measures, a range of existing sector-specific commitments benefit the creative industries.

Channel 4 has agreed to relocate staff and spending outside London, supporting jobs and gross value added (GVA) growth in new locations, stimulating new investment and TV production as the supply chain responds.

Last year almost £70m of public money was invested via government grant in aid and National Lottery funding through the British Film Industry (BFI) to support a range of activities across the UK, including film production, skills development and cultural promotion. Of this, approximately 65 per cent was spent on supporting activities outside of London.

Scope to go further

But we wish to further harness the creative talents of communities and make sure that the prosperity of the creative industries is felt across the UK.

We will commit £20m to establish a Cultural Development Fund (CDF) that will deploy investment to promote growth and prosperity for all. The fund will run over two years and will invest in areas of the country that can demonstrate high-impact, robust plans for using investment in cultural and creative industries assets to further economic growth and support local communities. Bids will be expected to demonstrate how they are match-funding the investment, including with significant private-sector investment. The creative industries will need to ensure that they play a prominent role in making these bids as strong as possible. Bids will need to outline specific commitments – including match-funding – in areas such as capital investment, physical space, new cultural and creative programmes, events and activities to enable the development and scale-up of local areas and businesses. This programme cannot work top-down.

Industrial Strategy Creative Industries Sector Deal

Industry will play a vital role in supporting the CDF by developing a programme of activity to promote businesses in specific areas outside London. This includes industry delivery of a Creative Kickstart programme to provide mentoring and advice on sector-specific issues around finance, branding, advertising, marketing, communications, exports and IP. This will be allied to an annual Creative Industries Roadshow, which will bring creative businesses together across clusters to network and exchange best practice.

As well as investment, there is a need for advocacy and support to help local areas with strengths in creative business learn from each other on how to drive growth using leadership, planning, procurement and other tools.

Building on the consultative approach to the Sector Deal, government will convene a Creative Local Industry Partnership to enhance collaboration between creative industries consortia, including the Creative Industries Federation, Creative Industries Council, Local Enterprise Partnerships, Combined Authorities and partners in Devolved Nations. Together, these parties will inform the creative aspects of Local Industrial Strategies – such as interventions to grow local creative sector strengths or harnessing creative industries to address the Grand Challenges that places are developing with government. This includes the forerunner strategies in development with partners in Greater Manchester, West Midlands and the Oxford–Milton Keynes–Cambridge growth corridor.

We will help areas reflect the aspirations and great economic potential of their creative businesses. The network will be to share good practice and support local leadership across the UK.

Alongside all these measures, other steps in this Sector Deal will support leading clusters including:

- The Arts and Humanities Research Council's Creative Industries Clusters Programme – enabling UK universities and creative businesses to address regional sector challenges through tailored research.
- Business support – given their links with the creative business community, creative clusters can house business support programmes, facilitate conversations between investors and businesses, inform investment decisions or sign-post tenants to other advice that is available.
- Creative careers – creative clusters bring together regional businesses, education providers and – critically – creative people. Within clusters lies a wealth of knowledge on career pathways, skills supply and employment demand; all are essential components to a successful careers programme.

Source: www.gov.uk/government/publications/creative-industries-sector-deal/creative-industries-sector-deal-html

These policy priorities reflect a broad range of activities across the creative sector. The need to focus on such diverse areas of the sector as exports, intellectual property, training and employment, and the need to drive growth demonstrate the scope and scale of government investment in the creative sector as a part of UK Industrial Strategy. In addition, the need to focus on the regions and growth in terms of training, employment and the development of the creative sector in a greater number of areas across the UK emphasises the importance of the sector to achieving economic development initiatives, also in terms of the post-Brexit landscape across the UK, and particularly in the English regions. The investment in the creative sector in the English regions, and across the devolved nations, would act as a potential replacement for European Union funding such as Horizon 2020 and the European Regional Development Fund (ERDF). Indeed, there is a strong focus in the UK Government strategy to work with universities as partners, and for these relationships to underpin the need for skills and training. These aspects are unpacked in Box 4.2, again taken from the UK Government'sCreative Industries Sector Deal.

As the policy priorities set out in the two boxes demonstrate, there is a core focus on the creative sector by the UK Government in terms of investment, and there is a longer-term focus on delivering training and skills to foster job creation across the broad church of the creative sector. The focus on working with universities and developing skills and job creation across the creative sector, as well as an expanded emphasis on distribution of funding towards the regions, means a longer-term drive towards both skills and employment. The shorter-term investment in a broad range of the creative economy, including aspects from gaming, digital medias, to the role of museums, heritage and galleries shows the emphasis on growth across the sector. In terms of growing the £84.1 billion that the creative economy is currently worth to the UK economy (DCMS, 2018), the focus of the Creative Industries Sector Deal demonstrates the Government's longer-term commitment to growth across the creative sector. Moreover, these goals are key aspects of economic development and renewal. Most particularly, the drive to deliver a greater number of creative jobs and growth across the creative sector ties it to core underpinning aspects of economic development and renewal, through employability, skills and training, and the focus on regions. The question of funding in the regions, to deliver economic development, growth and skills, is evidently made more pressing given the ongoing complexities of the Brexit negotiations. Though this is by no means confined to the creative sector, the need to plan for investment in growth sectors, future employment and skills, and the regions is a core part of the UK Government's planning for the creative sector.

The creative sector, economic development and the Brexit environment

The creative sector represents an area of potential large investment from the UK Government in the post-Brexit landscape. In investing in economic development and the regions, the creative sector has been an area of focus in terms of the digital economy, film, video games and heritage. To be sure, the need for the investment in skills, training and the regions is evident in the light of the fact that several of the cities or regions with the highest leave votes in the 2016 EU referendum, such as South Yorkshire or the South West, were also the highest recipients of EU funding: drawn from grants such as the European Regional Development Fund (ERDF) and European Social Fund (ESF), including Objective One funds. A key challenge for government in the post-Brexit landscape will be to ensure that infrastructure and projects within the creative sector, such as business development, digital start-ups or gaming, are still supported by funding. Within this broad challenge, there are three underlying aspects. First, the need to invest in areas where communities felt disenfranchised from decision-making and funding, even where these areas received high levels of EU funding; second, the need to ensure a fair distribution of funding between urban and rural areas in terms of the creative economy; and third, the need to engage communities in the creative sector through participation in skills, training and the arts to drive the economic development process and identify further priorities for spend and development. In the post-Brexit landscape, funding may be sourced from, perhaps, private-sector investment or government spend in these areas. Evidently, the three aspects of economic development in the creative sector identified here underline the need for community engagement mechanisms as well as growth to ensure renewal and development through this investment in these regions, while addressing long-standing economic and social issues such as inequality through the creative sector, and ensuring that economic development is visible, sustainable and enduring.

In questions of how to replace this funding, the UK Government is currently engaged in discussions for potential opt-ins to streams such as Erasmus+ funding, and has recently tabled the UK Shared Prosperity Fund and the Renewal Fund for cities. However, this also raises questions around the distribution of funds to city regions by differing political parties and their view of the creative sector, as well as how strategic priorities are set and by (and for) whom. Will such funding simply reflect the ideological party-political objectives of the incumbent UK government, and will the creative sector remain as a core policy focus in Industrial Strategy and wider policy thinking? The focus on funding in the regions for the creative sector would also demonstrate central government commitment to the longer-term role of the creative sector in economic development. The roles of foreign direct investment (FDI) in the creative sector and of small and medium-sized enterprises (SMEs) in driving economic development are also likely to be key in maintaining growth and success in the existing areas of strength across the creative sector, such as digital platforms, and the gaming industry. The creative industries are a core area of growth and of driving skills and jobs across places where there are existing strengths in the creative economy, such as the M4 corridor or London and the South East. Moreover, the creative sector is also a potential driver for renewal and community engagement through skills, training, and still fast-moving new skills for a changing economic and social environment. The creative economy, certainly through digital media, is also a core focus for local investment and growth, such as Greater Manchester Mayor Andy Burnham's digital strategy. The direction of travel, nationally and locally, reflects the need to invest in areas of established strength in the creative sector but also as a longer-term skills opportunity that reflects a broader policy agenda than only focusing on growth.

In terms of governance, the last ten years have seen marked changes to the regional landscape, with the South West undergoing some stark pain in the face of sharp and deep cuts to public sector and local authority funding. We must also consider the role of time. The temporal aspect of the creative sector in the UK has shifted towards a national-level focus on creativity as a driver for economic development. As examined earlier in this chapter, the UK Government has set out both short- and long-term policy goals to achieve development through the creative sector. In so doing, these agendas are seeking to draw together a broad array of activities across the creative sector, and use these areas as mechanisms for growth and development across a number of themes. These are aimed at increasing areas of success in education, skills and training; technological and digital innovation; and SME development. These kinds of activities are aimed at growing longer-term growth in the sector and an increased number of creative sector jobs and exports. In the shorter term, the UK Government's policy agenda shows investment in particular in education and skills across the creative sector. The creative economy as a driver for economic development has also benefitted from, as noted earlier in this chapter, various EU funding streams. The UK's policy agenda will need to capture the regional element of this funding in order to achieve the desired goals of education and training, and bridging the urban-rural gap.

As the UK national-level policy agenda moves towards capturing and growing the creative sector, the roles of the regional and local remain vital in realising growing employment in the creative sector, and in engaging communities with creative activities more broadly. The South West as a region has been dependent on the visitor economy in some areas, such as Devon and Cornwall, but also more generally on the role of public sector organisations that have traditionally been large employers across the region. These jobs have historically been located in some of the sectors that suffered the largest cuts during the austerity era, particularly across the healthcare sector, the education sector and the uniformed services – especially the army, navy and the police. Moreover, the region has undergone the problem of younger people leaving the area in search of employment opportunities elsewhere. As young people complete their studies and finish University, they relocate and the resident demographic becomes older. Moreover, these demographic challenges and the shifting governance landscape created more pressure on existing third-sector and community-facing groups. The regional governance architecture shifted from the established Regional Development Agencies (RDAs), which were abolished, to the newly convened Local Enterprise Partnerships (LEPs). This changing architecture at the regional level can be seen as a forerunner to the combined authorities and city regions. However, prior to the current regional governance landscape in the UK, the role of the regions was driven by the shift to LEPs and Enterprise Zones from RDAs. Local authorities in areas like Plymouth were facing rapidly and deeply reduced budgets in trying to deliver services. The Plymouth case study, moreover, shows us a context of austerity cutting into the traditional employment landscape. The role of community-facing groups, such as Take A Part examined below, became more pressing.

Practically and conceptually, there are governance and policy challenges here. The ned to engage communities in the agenda for driving the creative sector risks several of the barriers that economic development programmes have tried to overcome in other areas. For example, the need to be visible in the goals of the economic development projects; the need to be consultative in order to foster community engagement; and perhaps most importantly of all, the need to underpin the economic development programme with the sense that it is not being done to communities, rather with them. In practical policy terms, there are tensions between the top-down government policy of driving economic development through investment in the creative sector and the community-facing creative arts group. Why is this important? First, the national-level policy goals of the *UK Creative Sector Industries Deal* may replicate aspects of the community engagement, and may suffer from the longer-term realisation of the policy goals. For example, these goals may be prone to party political change nationally, as well as the need to ensure funding from Westminster to the regions, most pressingly in replicating current EU funding streams that enable the creative sector to drive economic development.

Conceptually, there are also policy challenges. Foremost among these is the potential for unresolvable tensions between the formal national level of governance that seeks to deliver economic development through investment in a broad range of strands of creative activities, and community-facing creative arts groups. Such groups tend to occupy policy spaces in an informal fashion, and may be campaign organisations or activists. That is, they are outside the established formal institutional and governance arenas. This has the potential to create a tension between the top-down and bottom-up aspects of the creative sector, which may frustrate community engagement and the kind of behaviour change needed to engender a greater level of community engagement. In terms of the role of these community-facing creative arts groups, the chapter now moves on to examine the UK case study in depth.

Creative arts organisations, renewal and economic development

The chapter now moves on from the national level to the local, in focusing on the case study of Take A Part (TAP). TAP is a creative arts organisation that works with communities and partners such as schools, charities and local government to foster community engagement and participation in the creative arts. The second half of the chapter gives an overview of the broader picture of economic development and renewal in the Plymouth area, before then moving on to examine the roles of TAP, the creative arts organisation focused on in this chapter.

The regeneration of Plymouth, in the south-west of England, aims to deliver growth and regeneration of environmental, social, housing and educational facilities across the city and its environs. This chapter examines changes to governance and project outcomes in the regeneration of Plymouth, focusing on communities, job creation and housing. Examining the governance structure in the area, and the roles of these key actors, the chapter draws upon theories of democratic leadership and uses governance frameworks to examine changes following the abolition of the RDAs and similar agents, such as that of private-sector actors. The chapter illustrates the progress of the projects thus far and the actors, which delivered these, and examines the changing nature of governance in regeneration in Plymouth.

Solving or tackling urban regeneration issues has been the focus of successive governments in the UK and globally, through varying policy agendas and ideological approaches. Most recently, we have seen the transition from large-scale partnership arrangements as illustrated by the new public governance paradigm, to a vision of business-driven community engagement to deliver regeneration. E. M. Forster's essay 'Two Cheers for Democracy' offers two timely reminders of the public good of democratic systems: first, that democracy allows variety, and second, that it can admit its mistakes. This chapter sets out to ask the same question of localism, using the example of urban regeneration programmes driven by the localism agenda in the city of Plymouth in the south-west of England.

Regeneration of Plymouth in these projects began under the New Labour administrations, in common with many regeneration programmes across England and the wider UK as the New Deal for Communities (1998) and the Sustainable Communities Act (2003) focused upon renewal of housing, education and communal spaces. We will focus on and examine the progress of these projects and the key funders, engaged in delivery, before examining the differing roles of these actors in governance of regeneration in Plymouth. The chapter will then conclude with a discussion of the changes to governance in regenerating Plymouth, revisiting the discussion of the abolition of the RDAs and other large non departmental bodies, and whether this has brought about a much more central role for the private-sector firms engaged in delivery of regeneration.

Though there has been some discussion in the literature of regeneration projects in the UK (inter alia, John, 2017; Allmendinger and Haughton, 2009; Brownhill and Carpenter, 2009; Raco *et al.*, 2008; Davies, 2002; Henneberry and Guy, 2000), a large amount of literature has been produced by agencies and the local level (Heart of Efford, 2015; Plymouth Community Homes, 2011; The Comprehensive Spending Review, 2010; Succession Strategy, 2009; The Mackay Vision, 2005) as well as central policy goals to reduce expenditure on agencies in areas like regeneration and, in so doing, dramatically reduce the centre's expenditure on large non-departmental delivery bodies, most relevant in this instance, the RDAs (HM Treasury, 2010). This chapter builds on the existing literature by setting out to discuss and examine projects, resources and governance in Plymouth, drawing on primary data and examining the relations between actors in the region, the impact projects for renewal and the impact of financial cutbacks on these projects.

The economic and social context for urban development and renewal

The wider context for urban development and renewal in the city of Plymouth is examined in the sections below, focused on a range of regeneration projects. The population over the last decade, concomitant with the lifespan of many of the regeneration projects in the city and surrounding areas, has risen, perhaps helped by the success of Drake Circus shopping centre and students coming to the area in order to study. Plymouth, as highlighted in recent research undertaken following a further rise in A-level passes, performs poorly in terms of its educational attainment, allied to the 4,900 residents with no formal qualifications (all ages 18 to 64). The following sections discuss the projects in Plymouth.

The focus of the ladder of participation in this chapter demonstrates the importance of TAP building trust within the local community in order to facilitate a governance process where the community scales the ladder of participation through engagement with TAP and its creative arts projects. The governance of regeneration and the role of communities within this have tended to focus upon 'the use of partnerships and networks in governance (design and delivery) of regeneration, development and community engagement programmes' (Shand, 2013: 21). The relationship between these actors is examined and, drawing upon a behavioural

Box 4.3 Take A Part's approach

Take A Part's approach is two-fold:

1. Commissions

We deliver on larger, risk-taking, artistic commissions with collaborators and stakeholders either citywide or community-focused.

2. Consultation and education

We also offer spontaneous short-term projects, which utilise arts as a vehicle to draw attention to issues, undertake consultation, help relay ideas and introduce creative processes to a community.

Take A Part's process benefits communities in several key areas:

- community planning and strategy
- green and blue space access and improvements
- health and wellbeing
- heritage
- young people

Key commissions

Nowhereisland Radio (2012) – Artists worked with five island communities across Plymouth to create five radio stations looking at what it meant to be a citizen of their local community. This was a response to the Nowhereisland project for the UK Cultural Olympiad. The station also focused on the creation and performance of a dystopian play about the future of Plymouth underwater as climate change continues. This was recorded live in communities with Foley sound.

www.effordtakeapart.org.uk/nowhereisland/

In Praise of Trees (2012) – An international sculptor was invited to work with the community of North Prospect and their green space, Ham Woods, to intervene in the space and create a spot for reflection, focus and play. Working with the history of the local area, he devised a sculptural seat that reflected the loss of an ancient oak on Christmas Day 2011, which was the beginning of a community myth. Through storytelling, maquette-making, studio visits and workshops, the community developed a voice and ownership and solidified a group that today continues to fundraise and commission for their local woodland – Friends of Ham Woods.

www.effordtakeapart.org.uk/in-praise-of-trees/

Grow Efford/Shed On Wheels (2008–2016) – Born out of a pilot project looking at gap sites and wild foods, a local artist worked over a long period with the residents of Efford to look at ideas of exchange, healthy eating and changing green spaces. Grow Efford is about planting, harvesting, cooking and eating together and developed into a social enterprise that runs to this day – The Allotment Project. The Grow Efford movement also supported a bespoke vehicle to share the process developed in Efford across the city, leading to peer-to-peer-led projects like Grow Efford.

www.effordtakeapart.org.uk/grow-efford-2009-2011/
www.effordtakeapart.org.uk/grow-efford-present-work/
www.effordtakeapart.org.uk/shed-on-wheels/
http://effordtakeapart.org.uk/greenorchestra/

Crazy Glue (2009–2015) – A schools-based after-school arts club based out of High View School in Efford, Crazy Glue built up from stop animation workshops through Go and See events to run Plain Speaking Tour peer-to-peer invitations for the city of Plymouth's hard-to-reach areas of residents to interact with British Art Show 7. The group also co-curated Efford: The Capital of Culture for Plymouth and is currently working on a multi-site exhibition for Plymouth with Foreground.

www.effordtakeapart.org.uk/effordthe-capital-of-culture-for-plymouth-2/

Source: www.effordtakeapart.org.uk/about/, 2019

Box 4.4 Impact of Take A Part

Figures

In 2014–2016, Take A Part:

- employed 85 artists for 410 days
- created 35 new commissions
- delivered 99 separate education sessions
- created an audience of 400,900 in Plymouth

Community planning and strategy

Efford is where Take A Part began, and the area is enjoying the legacy of the work we've done there.

- Efford's Building Community Initiative was awarded a Creating Excellence Award in 2010 for the work of involving arts in planning
- In 2006, Efford was registered as the fifth most deprived area in Plymouth; as a result of the regeneration work it is now the twelfth
- Social enterprises and community arts groups created by TAP are still running today: The Allotment Project, Crazy Glue and Magic Hour

Take A Part worked with the residents of Whitleigh on the Whitleigh Big Local project. In 2012 Whitleigh was awarded £1 million to improve the community. Take A Part projects managed to:

- pull together a strong board of people to manage how the £1m is spent and managed
- create community-wide understanding of the Big Local project and gave residents from all areas the opportunity to feed directly into it

In Barne Barton we've been supporting the community in their creation of a neighbourhood plan, the first to be completely community-led in the whole of Plymouth. We also:

- commissioned 'The Dividing Line' in partnership with the River Tamar Project, creating a narrative for the community's history and setting the community's access issues directly into an international film festival
- are currently working on the co-commissioning of an artist-designed bridge at Kinterbury Creek (Mudcott) to improve access to the only accessible shoreline on the estate

Green and blue spaces

Connecting the communities of Plymouth with the green and blue spaces around them is a big part of Take A Part's work.

Much of the work in Efford has been tied to the communities' green spaces.

- Take A Part helped to create a new social enterprise, which is still running today – The Allotments Project
- The Little Patch of Ground, a project in collaboration with Encounter, taught the community permaculture principles as well as developing their creative skills

In Barne Barton Take A Part has:

- devised a new community arts organisation – BBROOTS – to look at green space, blue space and the history of the area
- supported new works in local green spaces such as murals and exhibitions
- commissioned The Dividing Line Partnership with The River Tamar Project, a film that examines the community's relationship with their natural surroundings
- Began work to improve access to the community's green and blue spaces with the commission of a bridge at Kinterbury Creek

In support of the regeneration work being undertaken in Ham Woods, Take A Part worked with Stepping Stones to Nature and The Friends of Ham Woods to develop a sculptural commission.

- An internationally renowned artist was appointed to create the sculptural piece that would be set into the restored dry-stone wall.
- The process was an interactive one, giving the community ownership of the work. The community selected the artist, and visited his workshop in order to gain greater insight into the sculpture.

- The sculpture and the work of Friends of Ham Woods won the Pride of Plymouth Award in 2014 for best community project.

Health

In Efford, Take A Part started the Grow Efford project. Grow Efford is working with the Public Health Development Unit to develop opportunities for people in Efford to eat healthily and in a sustainable way.

- Efford Library now supports Grow Efford to maintain their green space as an edible public garden.
- Grow Efford secured ownership of a section of the community allotment and are working with local growers to develop the plot as a community growing plot.
- 75 new fruit trees were planted in Efford Valley in 2012.
- Grow Efford support regular events such as apple pressing, wild-food walks, juicing and chutney making.
- Take A Part commissioned the Shed on Wheels Project. A converted 1970s milk float that can be used as a meeting space and kitchen, the Shed on Wheels has been used across the city to promote green growing, sustainability and healthy eating.

Young people

Engaging the young people of the communities Take A Part work with is an important part of the Take A Part process. Moreover, it is incredibly important in securing the future both of those communities and of the arts themselves.

Take A Part's work in Efford has had great benefits for the young people of the community and has engaged them in a variety of ways; from a young persons' library group, Headspace, to social enterprising, stone carving and arts groups. The legacy as a result of this work is:

- Take A Part created the young persons' art group Crazy Glue, who have worked across the city and continue to thrive. They supported city-wide engagement in British Art Show 7.
- Take A Part supported High View School to achieve outstanding Ofsted (2012), Arts Mark Gold (2013) and UK Literacy School of the Year (2014).
- Take A Part created a school-based social-enterprise-creating film – *Magic Hour*. They have been commissioned by Take A Part, Plymouth City Council and other arts organisations to create films.
- Take A Part has created radio stations run by young people in Efford.

Through BBROOTS, Take A Part works with young people in the Barne Barton community.

- School children in Barne Barton worked on a project to name the streets in their community. The schoolchildren researched historical figures with relevant history or ties to the area and chose ones to name streets after.
- Currently Take A Part is working on a commission to build a bridge at Kinterbury Creek. To this end, Take A Part are working with the young people of the community to shape all aspects of the project.

In Stonehouse, Take A Part work with several groups including Stonehouse Action and Stonehouse Timebank and have worked to engage young people in a variety of ways.

- In preparation for the Union Street Party, Take A Part liaised with an artist to work with the children of Cathedral School St Mary.
- Artists ran workshops in Stonehouse schools working with the children to create lanterns. These lanterns were carried through the streets of Stonehouse in the Parade of Lights, which over 200 locals attended.

Heritage

Often, it is history that holds people together. Our work helps communities rediscover that history as well as build a new one together.

In Barne Barton, Take A Part have worked with the people of the area to build a sense of shared history and heritage.

- Take A Part's film commission *The Dividing Line* explores the ways in which the River Tamar has shaped the lives of the people of Barne Barton, and identifies access to the river as another step towards their heritage.
- Take A Part set up the community group BBROOTS who worked with local schoolchildren to research and rename the streets of the area.

In Stonehouse, Take A Part has explored the heritage of the area in several ways.

- Take A Part worked with Stonehouse Timebank to create the Stonehouse Seedstore. Lead artist Anne Marie Culhane collected 100 stories about individuals' relationships to plants through growing and eating. The Seedstore also includes plants that are, or have been, important in the story of Stonehouse.
- The highly successful Parade of Lights in November 2014 engaged the community in the creation of lanterns and through the parade itself. The event was part of the celebrations of the Three Towns Festival, remembering the joining of the three towns and their history.

Training opportunities

Plymouth University
Via a partnership with Plymouth University, Take A Part have offered several training opportunities to young people in Plymouth through internships both to students and recent graduates.

Plymouth College of Art
Take A Part worked with Plymouth College of Art in 2013/14 to create an exhibition of art in Barne Barton and exhibitions about Barne Barton both in the local community and the College.

Source: www.effordtakeapart.org.uk/about/, 2019

governance approach, it argues community-based organisations and institutions have assumed governance roles and developed close ties and trusting relationships with the communities within which the projects are undertaken.

Governance, partnerships and networks in regeneration

This section focuses on the key actors in governance and how the creative sector can drive economic development and urban renewal. Through various policy agendas and ideological approaches, identifying and dealing with urban regeneration issues has been the focus of successive UK governments. While economic development programmes have retained consistent themes such as job creation, community engagement and education and training initiatives, in terms of governance we have seen the transition from large-scale partnership arrangements (Kort and Klijn, 2012; Liddle and Diamond, 2007; Chondroleou *et al.*, 2005) as illustrated by the new public governance paradigm, to a vision of localism-driven business and community delivery for economic development and regeneration.

Creative industries and regional economic development in the post-Brexit landscape

Scholarly debates around Brexit and post-Brexit governance across differing policy arenas will also be examined generally (inter alia, Henderson, 2017; Hunt and Minto, 2017; Wincott, 2017) and specifically related to EU funding in the regions (Bachtler, 2017). These organisations have undertaken regeneration projects, been responsible for community engagement within them and set targets and funding levels, linked to regeneration initiatives such as improving neighbourhood safety, physical education activities or other community-based programmes.

Regeneration in Plymouth

In renewal initiatives in the city, there is also a role for the community; though again, this is part of a much broader partnership delivery model. This allows participation, but also creates the space for a more direct and micro level of community participation, ownership in the delivery of regeneration projects and through the development of trust engagement. Indeed, the development of trust through engagement of communities in regeneration projects was a central aim of both Labour and Conservative administrations' policies, in common with other European renewal programmes, such as Germany's Social City and the role of community as manager in project delivery (Shand, 2013). The Devonport Regeneration Community Partnership (DCRP), located in a historically poor area of the city, with high crime rates and similar levels of social exclusion, was a key partner in the Devonport Guildhall project, working with the local authority and private-sector actors in delivery, as well as the funders.

Until its abolition in May 2011, the DCRP had been engaged in several projects – many of which were completed – in the Devonport area in relation to community, health, education and employment. Examples of these projects include improvement of CCTV; more police on the streets in the area; an inclusion for a youth project; and a stop-smoking service (Devonport Regeneration Community Partnership, 2011). The role of the DCRP in governance is set out in the following sections on findings, but the organisation has worked with, as noted earlier, a range of actors, and the area's regeneration was taken forward by the Devonport Regeneration Company, in partnership with the local-level and private-sector housing firms.

TAP is operating in a poor area, connecting residents and community groups to the creative arts, widening access to these pursuits. The key aspect in TAP's success in such endeavours is the visibility of the organisation, and in the accessibility of what it is trying to engage people in. In terms of governance, this demonstrates a more straightforward approach to community working, rather than working with a raft of partners in a complex governance model, such as the ones discussed earlier in this chapter. TAP also commissioned a radio play in Efford that focused on the history of the area and was in addition to a range of activities in the community, such as running after-school clubs. This shows some important aspects of partnership working in delivery, mostly with the local authority, schools and the community. This is a far less complex and more accessible system of governance than has been seen in economic development and urban regeneration projects (Shand, 2016, 2013). The success of TAP is not in the governance design: rather, it is in the relationship built with the community. In any project, which is consciously or unconsciously about regeneration and development, the role of engaging the community, and key individuals, is vital. It is very hard to achieve anything if the community, or at least key figures in the community, are not open to your ideas.

TAP is currently working with communities in Cheltenham, Exeter and Poole to think about long-term approaches, to model the Arts Action Group approach and to follow the process of committing to the long term. This is via the support of TAP acting as a catalyst and mentor for the work. But it is a slow process and needs careful brokering and a large set of soft skills to ensure that the work remains relevant. The process also needs to consider how succession is built in. With so many socially engaged regeneration projects, the largest question is one of when to let go. TAP in its first iteration was organic in how it grew. It was testing and growing, and a firm concept of succession was not built in. Letting go in Efford has never been achieved and this may be due in part to being there too long. In other Arts Action Group communities, such as Ham Woods in

North Prospect, a durational project of two years with the upfront statement that the process would be timely, resulted in the community understanding and taking from it the tools they needed and the support towards the ambition to go on and self-fundraise and select artists in the Arts Action Group model far beyond the initial engagement of TAP.

In order to roll out a TAP model though, most importantly, the right people need to be around the table – the community, the organisations and the local authority – because each have their power bases and skills that are needed to ensure that the process of socially engaged projects in regeneration are realised. There is only so much that one power source can achieve. Participatory projects in regeneration need all the players to drive high ambitions ahead. The role of TAP in Plymouth underlines this point – the importance of issues like participation by the community in Efford; the linkage with other organisations in the area; and the willingness to embrace local strengths, history and knowledge.

So why is what TAP does so innovative? First, it works with the community, not at the community. Looking at regeneration projects in the round, there are risks of being overly top-down whereby targets or partnerships are imposed on communities, which do not fit, or which people are unaware of; through allowing learning from the existing Heart of Efford community partnership, and through not being part of a larger more complex governance model which had been superimposed on the community. This relationship between TAP and the local community demonstrates the need to embed regeneration or development work in existing community networks and histories: the engagement with the community necessitates trust-building, and both short- and longer-term vision. In some cases, regeneration initiatives have been hard to navigate for communities, due to changes in governance delivery. In the case of Plymouth – and in common with several other areas – these changes occurred through cuts, austerity and the ideological shift from agency-led to business-led delivery, as discussed earlier. While budget cuts evidently presented large issues for TAP as creative arts, local authority and third-sector budgets have been cut, Arts Council England (ACE) committed to spending more than £170 million outside London. This was in the broader economic context of public-service cuts in the region to NHS, police and armed services, each long-standing, largest employers in the region, and the local level scrapping £3.5 million planned spending in 2010 following the Autumn statement.

The lack of complexity of TAP's partnerships in governance and delivery is a notable feature of its success and visibility. This can be demonstrated by a history of projects working with the local community: a broad range of projects, such as running a radio station in the area, sculpture, schools projects and the Crazy Glue project, which aimed to reduce vandalism and graffiti in the Efford area by working with people in the community to produce street art and murals, which have not been vandalised since they have been completed. This notion of community ownership, participation and identity is another key aspect of achieving success in regeneration which TAP has engaged with. The role of TAP staff has been an innovative one, and perhaps has become one of governance rather than creative arts – not as a partner in governance, but as the visible force of change and progress in a disadvantaged area.

The community and the creative arts are the focuses of TAP, and the success of engaging communities from Efford in art exhibitions and sculpture would be a brilliant achievement on its own. But the influence of TAP in the area has taken on a broader role – one of visibility, and one of what can be achieved: a focal point for the community and important parts of it, such as local schools as well as local artists. The innovative focus of TAP is reflected in the shift in delivery of regeneration in the area. Prior to these projects, the community in the Efford area had experienced attempts at regeneration that were not consultative or engaging.

Too often in the past, Efford people had had things done to them, even for them – usually by well-meaning 'officials' with the best of intentions – but not done by them or with them. Somebody else had always been setting the agenda. Here was a chance to get away from 'tick-box' clipboard questionnaires. No more 'consultations', simply seeking comments on plans, which had already been prepared! The hope, this time, was to embark on something different, to have a real say, for the first time, in the future of the neighbourhood (Heart of Efford, 2015: 3).

Such previous governance failures in design of regeneration projects in the area had failed to engage the community and had frustrated the progress of social and economic development in Efford. In terms of governance, the 'flat' approach to governance and delivery has removed barriers to participation for the community in regeneration. To be sure, there are elements of co-production or co-commissioning in this process; but the iterative manner in which the relationship has grown between TAP and the community is less formal, more focused on outcomes through projects rather than structures and complex governance partnership design.

Reframing the theory: the role of the creative sector in terms of institutions, governance and behaviour

The role of TAP in a de facto 'governance' role, in modelling and influencing behaviour such as participation in the creative arts, is vital and visible.

The role of the in-country partners is vital in achieving legacy through more sustainable practices and in developing these practices and behaviours through both their existing networks and networks which will be grown in the future.

Reframing New Public Governance: collaboration and delivery

The role of community engagement with the creative arts in the TAP case enables us to revisit the established notion of New Public Governance (NPG). The focus in the NPG approach of collaborative working between the local level and the third sector and the emphasis on network exchange relationships has been disrupted by the community empowerment example in Plymouth. In establishing the NPG approach, Osborne argues, 'the 'NPG is rooted firmly within organisational sociology and network theory' (2006: 382). In asserting the transitional phase of the New Public Management (NPM) to the NPG, Osborne goes on to argue the NPG represents a return to many aspects of the traditional Public Administration. This transition has been characterised by:

> [B]oth a *plural state*, where multiple inter-dependent actors contribute to the delivery of public services and a *pluralist state*, where multiple processes inform the policy making system. As a consequence of these two forms of plurality, its focus is very much upon inter-organisational relationships and the governance of processes, and it stresses service effectiveness and outcomes. Further, it lays emphasis on the design and evaluation of enduring inter-organisational relationships, where trust, relational capital and relational contracts act as the core.
>
> (Bovaird, 2006; Teicher *et al.*, 2006; cited in Osborne, 2006: 384)

These accepted positions have been, as noted above, conceptualised as pluralistic and network driven and are seen as drawing the bottom-up organisation – such as TAP – into the institutional arena. The recent shifts in governance approaches have seen, however, both an overlapping and a fragmentation of networks and this has resulted in a messy governance process. Changes to governance delivery have not produced inter-organisational working and focused delivery. Neither have they reflected an arena where organisational systems co-exist. Rather, the realities of everyday governance are messy, clumsily overlapping and prone to external shock. This also means a greater likelihood of mistrust in top-down institutional approaches and formal governance initiatives. This disrupts the established idea that 'elements of each regime can and will co-exist' (Osborne, 2010: 2, cited in Lindsay *et al.*, 2014: 194). However, it further disrupts the notion that, as Lindsay *et al.* go on to argue, 'there is unlikely to be a single, decisive moment of shift from NPM to NPG' (Lindsay *et al.*, 2014: 194). The NPG makes assumptions about the rationality of networks and organising mechanisms that are often facilitated by overlapping, nested irrationalities, and driven by informal relationships (Ayres, 2017) that have endured locally and nationally, through such phases.

What lessons can be drawn?

What lessons can we draw from the TAP case in terms of community empowerment? For example, there is the need to actively engage with communities through notions of co-creative or co-productive approaches, and to manage competing and overlapping existing identities. The role of institutional design is crucial in understanding the historical barriers to effective community empowerment. In federal settings, for example, there are often formal structures that enable greater community empowerment. We may also see overlapping competencies – such as in the German example – where the regional and national levels share aspects of policy competencies. The UK's long history of unitary governance has mitigated against a localism agenda and such a focus on community empowerment. However, we should also stress that in some contexts it is a notion of decentralisation, rather than devolution, that is framing our understanding of community engagement with the creative arts and with governance policy agendas more broadly.

The role of TAP in the post-institutionalism context: institutions without institutionalism?

Drawing on the TAP case study, we can see this as a demonstration of an organisation outside institutional arenas operating as a de facto governance institution. Though driven by funding from institutional arenas and through several partnership arrangements, such as at the local level and with schools in the area, TAP has maintained a presence outside traditional institutional walls and structures.

The role of TAP as a creative arts group, has in some aspects, mirrored that of the UK Government's policy agenda. TAP has fostered a wide participation in the creative arts across the city of Plymouth, engaging communities who have begun to drive, rather than merely follow, creative arts activities. The role of TAP has also demonstrated the ability of community-facing groups to use the creative arts as means of driving economic development. This has occurred through using creative arts fora and events to enable local people who have previously been disengaged from civic life to play an active part. Moreover, examples such as the radio station that was driven by the local community show ownership of the process. Vitally, and more broadly, however, the role of TAP has evolved into something more than a creative arts organisation. The relationship with the local community has become one that resembles a kind of quasi-governance. TAP's partnership with local schools, for example, has led to greater participation in students engaging with after-school clubs and creating exhibitions. And this, in its turn, has encouraged parents to adopt the same behaviours.

With this in mind, the conceptual importance of such a relationship requires close examination. Organisations such as TAP reside outside formal governance arenas, beyond institutional walls. Yet the relationship with the community has brought about progress in terms of participation, engagement and educational attitudes. The relationship between TAP and the local community is a prime example of the creative arts as a driver for urban renewal and economic development, one that has brought about these examples of increased engagement, participation and behaviour change. Yet established governance thinking suggests that groups outside the formal governance institutional arena inevitably move towards it, before reframing aspects of the formal rules of the game and integrating into the usual formal settings. However, the story of TAP leads us to revisit these assumptions. The relationships with the local community will inevitably be easier to facilitate and more organic than they could be between communities and national-level government. But are there lessons from the ways in which behaviour change was engendered through TAP and the creative arts activities? Conceptually, established theory leads us to think that once an organisation becomes part of a process (such as a single-issue campaign organisation) it will travel, through negotiation and friction, eventually into the formal established institutional processes of governance. Philosophically, post-institutional and post-structural theory emphasises the notion of institutional structures as ever-evolving, moving beasts (Panizza and Miorelli, 2013), which can be reflexive and adaptable. In this way, they are able to admit new actors and ideas into the formal established settings (Glynos and Howarth, 2007: 139, cited in Panizza and Miorelli, 2013: 309). For institutional thinkers, the logic then follows that these formal established governing arenas must reorganise the institutions to drive progress and reflect societal changes. This approach, however, demonstrates the problem of the successful role of creative arts organisations in engaging and sustaining relationships with communities that empower and engage through the means of the creative arts and into wider civic life. While remaining outside formal governance arenas, agents are able to challenge established institutional norms. Over time, these agents then move from outside these formal governance settings to eventually move inside the institutions, becoming part of the institutional fabric themselves. For Hay, this leads to an environment where time is key (Hay, 2001: 203, cited in Panizza and Miorelli, 2013: 309):

> Time within this [institutional] framework is textured and contoured, alternating (though in no preordained or predetermined manner) between decisive, intense and contested moments of crisis and paradigm shift on the one hand, and longer, slower, more drawn out periods of iterative change and path dependent institutional evolution on the other.

Equally, there remains the disruptions and tensions between the established institutional focus on participation, funding and employability and the bottom-up more agent-driven role of creative arts organisations in driving community engagement in participation. The role of TAP as a go-to organisation for the local community, we can argue, owes much to its position outside these formal governance arenas. The distance between the community and decision-makers, as we have noted through Sorensen's work, can be exaggerated by the complexities and multi-levelled nature of governance. Moreover, the feeling among communities that economic development and urban renewal is done to them rather than in conjunction with them is a major barrier to sustainable urban renewal and economic development initiatives. Moreover, the kinds of behaviour change we have seen in the TAP case study have shown the ability of informal groups outside the governance arena to act as a de facto governance organisation. TAP has facilitated improved relationships between community actors and behaviour change, demonstrated through the creative arts.

Concluding remarks: the role of TAP and the community in delivering regeneration differently

This chapter has examined the role of TAP in engaging the community through participation in creative arts projects to achieve regeneration and has focused upon this in the context of progress, funding and governance of regeneration in Plymouth. The projects and broader governance of regeneration in Plymouth have, in common with the shifting focus of the centre, moved towards a more private-sector-driven model. The shift from large top-down agency delivery, through austerity and the focus on the private and voluntary sector, has created greater need and space for organisations such as TAP to work with communities, and the local community has clearly engaged. Through engaging with TAP and participation in various local economic development projects, the community has begun to drive, design and deliver regeneration projects of its own in the area.

In terms of austerity, the main changes in terms of governance are in the effect this has had on the projects of regeneration in the city. The focus of housing and job creation had begun to move towards a more profit-enhancing motive, rather than social need. This again created social factors and the need for TAP to engage with the community through creative arts projects, to address regenerative goals such as a focus on education, crime prevention and community engagement. The evidence of communities engaging and delivering projects with creative arts organisations such as TAP suggests that communities feel divorced from both agency-led and business-driven regeneration projects, pointing the way towards more community-driven, co-produced and sustainable delivery.

Overall the community has moved from a non-participatory position to one of citizen power – or grassroots participation driven by engagement, ownership and the sustainability of projects and community. Larger-scale regeneration projects often fall prey to didactic top-down targets or complex systems of delivery, meaning the community may be consulted at the implementation stage rather than engaged in design, co-production or co-commissioning of projects, reflecting the stage of degrees of tokenism: typically placation, consultation and informing. However, the increase in community participation and the subsequent work on combating aspects of anti-social behaviour such as graffiti can be viewed as a result of the development of a climate of trust. This was underpinned by co-produced and consultative methods that fostered citizen participation and indeed partnership with the community as well as with formal governance mechanisms and through existing networks and funded projects. Fundamentally, TAP activities and strategies identify a 'continuum of participation' between instrumental and grassroots levels of participation whilst ascending Arnstein's ladder of participation (Silverman, 2005; Arnstein, 1969).

In arguing the case that TAP disrupts established institutional thinking, the role of TAP is a problem in terms of accountability. While, undoubtedly, the organisation has been a driving force in aspects of renewal and economic development, it is not accountable, or legitimised (in the traditional sense of being elected), and could simply walk away from the types of projects examined in this chapter. This problem creates practical and conceptual questions. First, practically, the findings underpinning the idea of TAP as an organisation can be seen to be filling in a governance gap. TAP has acted as a focal point for communities, which have reached beyond their creative arts remit, and become a point of contact for communities around issues such as education and participation. This raises – as noted in the theoretical discussion earlier – practical and conceptual questions. TAP is not responsible or formally representative of communities, its members are unelected and it is not a third-sector organisation. This shows the importance to TAP of a type of informal governance (Ayres, 2017). The question of austerity also comes into play here. The projects driven by TAP in Plymouth have been undertaken in the post-2009 landscape; it is an area that has been heavily dependent on public services in terms of employment, and the cuts to these services have had a large impact on the city. In terms of economic development, TAP has been increasingly 'filling in the gap' of the local level and third sector, despite having no formal accountability or legitimacy; but – as noted earlier – it has been seen as a visible point of contact by local people.

As examined in this chapter, in terms of conceptual importance, this leads us to revisit established examples of institutional structures and the relationship with agency. In fostering roles and behaviours through working with the local level, schools and charities in the area, TAP has worked in partnerships with formal governance actors, but has remained outside the institutional arena. Indeed, it is occupying this space outside the established institutional arena that has made TAP so important as a point of contact for the community.

Conceptually, we have seen the blurring of established notions of structure and agency through the activity of TAP. Though operating in partnership with formal partners, such as local government, TAP's strength and success lies in fostering participation within the local community. This ability to represent a source of advice and support for communities while remaining outside traditional perceptions of established institutional walls and arenas has fostered a trust within less affluent communities. Top-down investment goals that attempt to drive community participation and bigger engagement with the creative arts have not enjoyed this level of success, and certainly not in such a way. The engagement with communities – and, equally importantly, the participation in creative arts that TAP has seen in Plymouth – demonstrates the role of TAP as a point of contact outside institutional walls. The importance of this success is not just practical. As discussed earlier in this chapter, this demonstrates conceptual disruptions to the established institutional and governance approaches. The governance approaches are disrupted by the role of TAP as a point of contact, acting as a de facto governing mechanism. Though working in partnership with public organisations, TAP maintained a presence outside the establishment. These disruptions extend to the structure–agency debate. The agency of TAP in acting as a bottom-up organisation achieving community participation and engagement in the creative arts has mirrored that of established institutions, but has been more successful in changing the behaviour of local communities in participating and engaging in the creative arts. The debates outlined in the institutionalism literature around agents eventually migrating into structures and becoming part of the establishment to become an institution are also disrupted by organisations like TAP. The ability of TAP to operate outside the traditional institutional and governance frameworks, and foster community engagement in the creative arts has also been a new means of 'doing' governance. As discussed in the New Public Governance sections earlier in this chapter, the established relationships of third-sector and local-level partnerships are again different to what we have seen with the TAP case – a small organisation that operates outside traditional structures, with partnerships enacted in an ad hoc fashion; yet TAP has demonstrated the capacity to engage with the community and to drive economic development and renewal projects through the creative sector in an area of low affluence.

References

Allmendinger, P. and Haughton, G. (2009) Soft spaces, fuzzy boundaries, and metagovernance: The new spatial planning in the Thames Gateway *Environment and Planning A* 41: 617–633

Arnstein, S. (1969) A ladder of citizen participation *Journal of the American Institute of Planners* 35 (4): 216–224

Bachtler, J. (2017) *Towards cohesion policy 4.0: Structural transformation and inclusive growth* Regional Studies Association Europe

Brownhill, S. and Carpenter, J. (2009) Governance and 'integrated' planning: The case of sustainable communities in the Thames Gateway, England *Urban Studies* 46 (2): 251–274

Chondroleou, G., Elcock, H. and Liddle, J. (2005) A comparison of local management of regeneration in England and Greece *International Journal of Public Sector Management* 18 (2): 114–127

Davies, J. (2002) The governance of urban regeneration: A critique of the 'governing without government' thesis *Public Administration* 80 (2): 301–322

Department for Culture Media and Sport (2018) *Britain's creative industries break the £100 billion barrier* London: DCMS

Devonport Regeneration Community Partnership (2011) www.devonportonline.co.uk/historic_devonport/articles/articles.aspx

Heart of Efford Community Partnership Magazine (Summer 2015)

Henderson, M. (2017) What works and why? Student perceptions of 'useful' digital technology in university teaching and learning *Studies in Higher Education* 42 (8): 1567–1579

Henneberry, J. and Guy, S. (2000) Understanding urban development processes: Integrating the economic and the social in property research *Urban Studies* 37 (13): 2399–2416

HM Treasury: The Comprehensive Spending Review (2010) London: HM Treasury

Hunt, J. and Minto, R. (2017) 'Between intergovernmental relations and paradiplomacy: Wales and the Brexit of the regions' The British Journal of Politics and International Relations 19 (4): 647–662

John, P. (2017) *How far to nudge? Assessing behavioural public policy* Cheltenham: Edward Elgar

Kort, M. and Klijn, E. (2012) Public-private partnerships in urban regeneration: Democratic legitimacy and its relation with performance and trust *Local Government Studies* 39 (1): 89–106

Liddle, J. and Diamond, J. (2007) Reflections on regeneration management skills research *Public Money & Management* 27 (3): 189–192

Lindsay, C., Osborne, S. and Bond, S. (2014) The 'new public governance' and employability services in an era of crisis: Challenges for third sector organisations in Scotland *Public Administration* 92 (1): 192–207

Osborne, S. (2006) The new public governance? *Public Management Review* 8 (3): 377–387

Panizza, P. and Miorelli, M. (2013) Taking discourse seriously: Discursive institutionalism and post-structuralist discourse theory *Political Studies* 61 (2): 301–318

Plymouth Community Homes News (2011) *Estate in Line for Makeover* Issue 7 Summer 2011

Raco, M., Henderson, S. and Bowlby, S. (2008) Changing times, changing places: Urban development and the politics of space-time *Environment and Planning A* 40: 2652–2673

Shand, R. (2013) *Governing sustainable urban renewal: Partnerships in action* Abingdon: Routledge

Shand, R. (2016) *The governance of sustainable rural renewal: A comparative global perspective* Abingdon: Routledge

Silverman, R. M. (2005) Caught in the middle: Community Development Corporations (CDCs) and the conflict between grassroots and instrumental forms of citizen participation *Journal of Community Development Society* 36 (2): 35–51

Sloan, L. and Shand, R. (2012) Regeneration vs. the market? How house prices in Barking were affected by urban renewal programmes *Social and Public Policy Review* 6 (2): 21–34

Succession Strategy (2009) Plymouth: DRC Partnership

The Comprehensive Spending Review (2010) London: HM Treasury

The Mackay Vision (2005) Plymouth: 20/20 Vision

Wincott, D. (2017) Brexit dilemmas: New opportunities and tough choices in unsettled times *The British Journal of Politics and International Relations* 19 (4): 680–695

www.drcpartnership.co.uk/projects

www.effordtakeapart.org.uk/nowhereisland/

www.effordtakeapart.org.uk/in-praise-of-trees/

www.effordtakeapart.org.uk/grow-efford-2009-2011/

www.effordtakeapart.org.uk/grow-efford-present-work/

www.effordtakeapart.org.uk/shed-on-wheels/

www.effordtakeapart.org.uk/greenorchestra/

www.effordtakeapart.org.uk/effordthe-capital-of-culture-for-plymouth-2/

5 Germany

From creative and cultural industries to Refugees' Kitchen

This chapter addresses the role of the creative sector in economic development in the German context. The chapter begins by investigating the institutional and governance context for the creative sector in Germany, initially by focusing on the role of national-level investment in the creative sector. The chapter will focus on core policy priorities, funding streams, timing of projects and the key intended outcomes from these policy goals. The chapter then moves on to examine the role of Berlin as an example of success in the creative sector driving urban renewal and development. The second half of the chapter then moves on to unpack the role of more bottom-up creative arts organisations in Germany, and critically discusses their role in economic development. The chapter then applies these findings to the conceptual frameworks, focusing on the implications for the established theoretical ideas of governance, institutions and behaviour. Finally, the chapter sets out the key conclusions and learning from the German case study for the creative sector and economic development.

Established debates

The creative sector has been well documented in the scholarly debates across a range of areas. Established scholarly debates show a wide-ranging examination of different aspects of the creative sector, such as trust (Radomska *et al.*, 2019); entrepreneurship and growth; and the German creative sector in comparative context of creativity (Park and Hong, 2019). Moreover, the comparative nature of the roles of creativity and communities has been examined by Darras (2019) and the importance of innovation driven by the creative sector in the German context has been examined in terms of global partnerships and knowledge transfer (Park and Hong, 2019).

The key roles of information and communication technology (ICT) and digital technologies as drivers within the creative sector are, as will be discussed in later sections of this chapter, core to policy goals of growth in the creative sector. The importance of these technologies in driving growth across the creative sector is central to job creation and developing longer-term skills, training and education. Moreover, the creative sector has been argued to be key to the growth of regions in Germany (Wedemeier, 2010), as well as the creative sector being a driver for growth in terms of employment in the regions in Germany (Mossig, 2011). Cities have been examined in terms of the policy history and investment focus in the creative sector. Power (2011) argues that the importance of Hamburg and Munich has been central to driving employment in these cities through the growth of the creative sector, and their emergence has been vital in delivering growth and employment outside Berlin. Moreover, the importance of cities as creative hubs acts as an important aspect overseas in terms of driving tourism and in driving the creative sector forward (Wyszomirski, 2004).

In terms of the historical context, there is a long precedent for the creative-political setting. McRobbie (2011) details the history of radical creative arts enterprises in Germany, focusing on the creative economy as a product of these radical movements. Indeed, the conceptual discussion of interchange in this context will be addressed in the latter sections of this chapter. The comparative context of the creative sector as a driver for growth and employment across Europe has been documented by Wiesand and Soendermann (2005), focused on the role of job creation.

The governance and policy context for the creative sector in Germany has a long and established history. The arts are well established as a means of protest and urban community politics. For example, the role of bohemian and counter-cultural movements in the 1970s saw Kreuzberg develop as an area of the arts. At the time, it was one of poor housing stock, high demand and poor standards of living. However, this decade also saw a turn towards a shifting demographic in Kreuzberg. The impact of high numbers of squatters in the area saw pressure on government to accommodate the growing numbers of artistic bohemian younger people who sought or occupied housing in areas of Kreuzberg. This period also saw the establishment of art, protest and a more radical approach to politics in Kreuzberg. From being an area of high and historic immigration, dating back to the Huguenots in the seventeenth century (Kil and Silver, 2006) Kreuzberg maintained an identity as an area of high immigration and housing demand into the 1970s and 1980s in the guest workers era. In the present day, Kreuzberg has become 'a young multinational mix [that] populates the neighbourhood and rules the economy. Properties in Kreuzberg are among the most valuable assets in Berlin' (Guthmann Estate, 2019). As Bader and Bialluch (2009) argue, this position is set in the context of two periods of urban renewal driven by national policy, and underpinned by the emergence and durability of the creative demographic resident in the area. The opposed sides of the gentrification question demonstrate a long-standing schism in governance, between the formal institutions – nationally, regionally and locally – delivering wider economic development programmes in Kreuzberg. However, within the campaign groups outside the institutional arenas there is also a splintered effect. The groups that have long been campaigning against gentrification in Kreuzberg are made up of art and creative groups, where historically there was not such a historical and pronounced demographic driven by the arts scene housing in the area. The differences in these groups are not products of the variations in institutional context. Rather, they have different responses to the problem of gentrification of housing and the negative effect this policy direction has had on the housing legacies of large-scale economic development programmes. Rather than a campaigning demographic that draws upon a bohemian art subculture, the emphasis has been very much on growth and development in economic development programmes. In each case, the complexity of governance arrangements in such initiatives places housing development as one aspect of several policy goals, such as improved access to jobs, digital technological improvements, greater green space and investment in education.

These tensions have led to ruptures in communities, both through physical changes in Kreuzberg, and to the demographics of resident communities. The issue of gentrification lies at the heart of these cases, to be sure; however, equally vital in understanding how these tensions have arisen is the notion of legacy. Economic development in the area has been informed by strategies of growth, and has been entwined with broader economic development initiatives in the German context, as discussed elsewhere in this chapter, such as the Socially Integrative City. The responses to these changes have led to shifting demographics with an affluent artistic community that, though long-standing in the area, remain unresolved. The fragmented nature of governance arises from, moreover, the large amount of actors engaged in delivery of economic development programmes. This complex mesh of actors leads to further distance between decision-making and communities. In the German context, the resistance to gentrification has failed to assuage the strain on housing demand. In terms of accountability, these issues of gentrification and legacy in Kreuzberg have led to increased activity and campaigns by anti-gentrification groups, fracturing the relationship between communities and local governance. The perceived lack of accountability in meeting housing demand and affordability has led to failures in legacy effects of urban economic development in Kreuzberg. The gentrification of the area in this case has increased divisions within already fragmented communities, and married the notions of art and creativity with an affluent demographic. In addition, this has created a fractured relationship with levels of governance. The issue with renewal of housing as part of economic development programmes demonstrates the sharp collision of politics and markets. The continued gentrification of housing as a driver for economic development has led to increased fragmentation and inequalities within Kreuzberg. The complex nature of governance processes involved in the delivery of large-scale economic development programmes, as discussed earlier in the chapter, also makes policy-makers more distant from communities.

Funding and delivery in the creative sector

What are the key organisations that drive the creative sector and what are the implications for economic development and governance?

The nature of governance in the creative sector in Germany is driven by three different levels of both governance and delivery. The funding programmes, which will be examined later on in this chapter in detail, focus on skills development and training, as well as embedding creativity at the heart of renewal and development. The national, regional and local levels each focus on the role of creativity in driving job creation, physical place-making and linkage to education, green space, tourism and cultural development. The following section sets out the key policy priorities and the core funders.

The funding for the creative sector in Germany is drawn from the supranational, national and regional levels. It is drawn from the public and private sectors, and is focused on projects such as SME development, job creation, training and skills development, growing exports and the importance of the creative economy in driving tourism. The multi-levelled nature of these funding arrangements is underscored by the large role of EU structural funds in creative sector projects in Germany.

Linkage to broader economic development and renewal

What is the role of creative arts organisations in economic development?

How does the creative sector align with the broader policy goals of economic development and renewal? Nationally, there has been a recent focus on the need to emphasise social cohesion, housing and green space. In addition, there is a clear focus on drawing upon strengths such as tourism, history and business development. Recent large-scale economic development and renewal initiatives nationally in Germany, such as the Socially Integrative City, have drawn upon the role of green space, educational programmes, building new housing and refurbishing existing housing stock, and community engagement. These broad focuses of economic development and renewal sought to deliver both short- and long-term solutions to long-standing social issues. The role of the creative sector is well established in Berlin as a means of transformation, in terms of physical change and social change.

Examining the key funders and projects in the creative sector, and its role in driving forward economic development, the governance picture is one of multiple tiers of funding. Projects and funders range from UNESCO, varying EU streams of funding and the national and regional levels of investment in the creative and cultural industries. This sets the governance and policy context for the national policy priorities across the

Table 5.1 Political economy of the creative sector in Germany

Project	Funders	Level of governance	Key partners	Political era
Cultural and Creative Industries Initiative	EU Structural Funds; Private sector; National level	Supranational; National; regional; local	UNESCO; EU	2007–
German Motion Picture Fund (GMPF)	EU Structural Funds; Private sector; National level	National (Federal Ministry for Economic Affairs; subsequently Energy Federal Government Commissioner for Culture and the Media; German Federal Film Board	German Federal Film Board	2015–

Source: www.bmwi.de/Redaktion/EN/Artikel/Economy/german-motion-picture-fund.html, 2020.

creative sector. The role of the national, regional and local levels in promoting and developing the creative and cultural sector is long established, and has yielded significant funding across the sector. Indeed,

> [a]long with measures at both Federal and *Länder* level to promote films, the German Federal Film Fund has provided an additional EUR 60 million (USD 88.5 million) each year since 2007. In order to preserve the diversity of the German film landscape, the Federal Government and the *Länder* have been funding the digitisation of smaller and less financially viable cinemas since 2011. Since 2003, the Berlinale Talent Campus has provided a forum for up-and-coming filmmakers, which has given rise to a vibrant worldwide network. The cultural and creative industries are among the fastest growing sectors in Germany, with some 244,000 enterprises, a workforce of over one million and a turnover of around EUR 137 billion (USD 183 billion) in 2010. They make a great contribution to the diversity of Germany's cultural landscape.
>
> (UNESCO, 2012: 4)

Moreover, the progress of projects across the creative and cultural sector has been marked by investment that promotes projects on sustainable development, diversity and growth. In this vein,

> [s]upport for international cooperation in the arts, music, theatre, dance, literature and film sectors is a significant part of Germany's

cultural relations and education policy. In 2010, financial resources totalling EUR 1.513 billion (USD 2 billion) were made available by the Federal Government for cultural relations and education policy measures. Advanced training programmes for publishers and publishing professionals from the Arab world run by the Frankfurt Book Fair in conjunction with the Goethe-Institut since 2006 have been particularly successful. Also noteworthy are Quantara.de, Deutsche Welle's online dialogue platform with the Arab world since 2003, and its Farsi-language online forum, launched in 2010. Over 240 million people around the world access Deutsche Welle via satellite and the Internet.

(UNESCO, 2012: 4)

Indeed, the creative and cultural sector was identified as a major focus of promoting the goals of diversity and inclusion in the Lisbon Treaty (2005), and the subsequent funding streams, such as the European Framework 7 projects and latterly Horizon 2020 funds. Moreover, the German context for investment and growth in the cultural and creative industries has been a focus for growth (Nathan et al., 2015: 5):

Germany's creative economy and creative industries are bigger than the UK's in counts – the only instance of this in the countries we consider – but are smaller in relative terms (7.96 per cent versus 9.93 per cent of the workforce in 2013). Both creative economy jobs (0.09 percentage points) and creative industries jobs (0.04 percentage points) have grown marginally between 2012 and 2013 ... Germany has more people employed in creative occupations (1.66 million) compared with the UK's 1.39 million, while creative industries employment is relatively similar: 2.26 million for Germany and 2.22 million for the UK. The German figures are based on slightly more recent data (2012–13 as opposed to 2011–13) which may also inflate them relative to the UK figures. As the German workforce has around ten million more people than the UK's, creative industries and occupations account for a larger proportion of the UK's workforce. Another difference is that creative occupations are more likely to be employed in creative industries (0.82 million) in the UK than outside the creative industries (0.57 million) in the EU LFS data, whereas in Germany the split is more even (0.81 million vs 0.85 million). The creative intensity of the UK (0.367) and German creative industries (0.357) are relatively similar.

Institutional and governance context

What are the key policy priorities for the creative sector?

The creative sector in Germany has been driven by the success of creative arts and the wider creative economy in cities such as Hamburg and Berlin, and has been a core driver for economic development across large-scale urban renewal initiatives. The governance setting for the creative sector in economic development in Germany has been one of overlapping regional and national competencies, across economic development policy goals such as improved housing, investment in employment, jobs and skills, green space and community engagement. The focus on investment in the creative sector in the German case has been driven by investment in and the development of existing areas of strength. In attempting to further develop these areas of the creative sector, the key areas of investment and growth are examined in the discussion below, as the music industry; the book market; the art market; the film industry; the performing arts industry; the design industry; the architectural market; the software and games industry; the press industry; and the advertising industry. In drawing upon such a broad church of creative activities, there is a rich opportunity to invest in areas of the creative economy that will deliver growth, employment and that can be buttressed by investing in skills, education and training for the sector. The following sections investigate the core policy priorities for the creative sector in Germany and set out these policy goals and the investments in this broad range of activities across the creative sector. The following empirical sections begin by examining the policy priorities at the national level, before moving on to focus on the levels of investment in the creative sector; they then move on to unpack the role of governance and strategic planning in Berlin, focused on the 2030 strategy and the central role of the creative sector in delivering growth and a creative city. The overlap across these areas in terms of governance and delivery is then examined. As noted elsewhere in this book, both Berlin and Hamburg have enjoyed considerable success over time as creative hubs. The role of policy priorities in the Berlin context – as set out in this chapter – focuses on sustaining job creation and growth over time, investing in the creative sector rather than fragmenting investment by focusing on one or two of the areas of activities across the sector (Shafi *et al.*, 2019; Herrigel, 2010; Schmidt, 2001).

National policy priorities

The following sections focus on the national-level policy goals, beginning with the national-level strategy for the German creative sector. The German policy strategy for the creative sector pulls together the cultural and creative aspects of the sector and acknowledges the vast nature of the sector. In seeking to harness this energy towards economic development and renewal more broadly, the focus on culture and creativity is a means of increasing productivity in the sector.

As noted earlier in the chapter, the creative sector in Germany covers a very broad range of activities. These are divided into eleven constituent strands, encompassing heritage-driven aspects as well as digital and gaming

---

Box 5.1 Creative and cultural growth

Cultural and creative professionals can be found in many areas of the economy, and are not limited to the (economic) categories defined in this chapter as belonging to the cultural and creative industries. For example, marketing and advertising jobs are also found in large financial service providers or in the automotive industry. On the other hand, there are tasks in the culture and creative industries that are carried out by individuals not belonging to this profession, for example administrative staff of a music publisher, or the custodian in an architectural office. In this section we will follow up on this perspective and will provide an overview of the tasks and professions involved in the culture and creative industries in Germany. Based on a model used in the UK, certain professions are defined as culture and creative professions. Using this differentiation, we can analyse the jobs in this professional group – for the entire economy, individual sectors and for the submarkets in the cultural and creative industries. Detailed data on employment provide the basis for this analysis. Compared to the traditional differentiation according to economic sectors, this data paints a more complete picture of employment in the culture and creative economy. In 2013, approximately 430,000 cultural and creative professionals with compulsory social insurance coverage or marginal employment were employed in the submarkets of the cultural and creative industries. Until 2015, this number grew to about 459,000 persons. This corresponds to an increase of the percentage of cultural and creative professionals in the cultural and creative industries of 2.5 percentage points, from 37.6 per cent to 40.1 per cent.

Source: www.bmwi.de/Redaktion/EN/Publikationen/monitoring-of-selected-economic-key-data-on-culture-and-creative-industries-2016.pdf?__blob=publicationFile&v=4

---

enterprises. These diverse branches of the creative sector are grouped together to aim at growth across both existing and developing areas of strength. In terms of economic development and renewal, these eleven aspects of the creative sector show a picture of growth and expansion across the sector. These core priorities represent a top-down approach to the creative sector, driving, over the longer term, sustainable economic development and expansion in the amount of jobs across the cultural and creative industries.

Looking at Box 5.2, the clear focus on growth and investment in the creative sector as a means of driving economic development is drawn across these eleven areas. The narrative of growth, moreover, is one that feeds into an already burgeoning sector.

The role of behaviour, institutions and agents

The chapter now turns to examine the policy goals set out in Box 5.3 in conceptual terms. In the German creative sector, certainly governance has been characterised by multiple levels of funding – driven by European

Box 5.2 Berlin Strategy 2030

Berlin 2030 will be a flourishing, broad-based international business location, the leading smart city in Europe and one of the most successful science and research regions in the world. It will be a source of new technologies and intellectual innovation. The city's technological dynamism, investment climate and cosmopolitan image will draw people and businesses from around the world, further strengthening the pull of the city. Berliners will have good jobs and the city will stand as a global example of how training and lifelong learning can create full employment. Training opportunities will be as international as the city: multilingual, diverse, enriching, genuinely inclusive. Berlin will be a city for all, promoting and demanding lifelong commitment across generations. As a creative centre for art and culture, as a tourist destination and as a sporting stronghold, the city will more than live up to its reputation as a global city. Berlin will inspire creatives from around the world, offering networks and spaces in which they can develop. It will in turn benefit from the creative spirit of these individuals as art, culture, fashion, media, sport and tourism forge a common identity across the diverse city, enhancing quality of life and building strong economic sectors.

Source: www.stadtentwicklung.berlin.de/planen/stadtentwicklungskonzept/
download/strategie/BerlinStrategie_Broschuere_en.pdf, 2019

Box 5.3 Developing 2030

Berlin 2030 enjoys an international reputation as a creative centre. Dynamic developments in art, culture, tourism and sport have increased its appeal and established its reputation as a global city. Berlin has an important role as a major city for artistic and cultural production with high-brow, independent, alternative and avant-garde performances created in Berlin being exported around the world. The creative environment is underpinned by a sound framework and plenty of open spaces where innovative works are staged alongside classics. Berlin's leading position on the international scene is confirmed by high-profile events including art, fashion and music fairs as well as major sporting events. Berlin's status as a global city has led to an increase in its appeal as a cultural and tourist destination. The success and quality of its productions and events spill over into international target markets, drawing audiences from around the world. Culture has become the lifeblood of Berlin and its inhabitants. The wide range of high-quality cultural provision in all fields, genres and formats influences quality of life in Berlin, which is also improved by healthy collaboration between the city and the cultural industries and by the use of sport as a vehicle for social inclusion. The increased value creation and coalescent value-creation chains of the creative economy, from culture and sport as well as tourism, have a knock-on effect on the manufacturing sector, contributing to economic growth and many types of innovation. Berlin offers opportunities and spaces for self-expression, development and innovation, which are supported by the city authorities whenever it is financially feasible, thereby maintaining a balance between culture and commerce.

Berlin enjoys a global reputation as 'the place to be'. Its unique atmosphere of freedom and tolerance draws people to the city from around the world, making diversity a Berlin trademark. People from different walks of life with very different life histories all aspire to living, working and realising their ideas and dreams in Berlin, making the city a testing ground of spaces, niches and historic divisions that offer an unparalleled environment for developing individual lifestyles and talents. This very special Berlin attitude to life is expressed in many ways, but particularly in the great breadth of cultural potential present in the city. Berlin promotes both individual creativity and community development. Intrinsic to Berlin are the many and varied opportunities to use and shape public spaces, which allow people to determine the future of their city. Culture acts as a trigger and a catalyst for essential social debate. Being a world-class sporting venue also guarantees Berlin both local and international pre-eminence. It offers an unrivalled wealth of sporting opportunities as well as the chance for each and every inhabitant to develop his or her sporting potential.

Berlin 2030 is a national and international benchmark for education and skills, key factors in employment, integration, prosperity and achieving equal participation. Anyone living in Berlin has every chance to make something of him- or herself – a promise delivered by providing equal access to educational opportunities for all sections of the Berlin population. Ensuring high-quality standards, education providers match the services they provide to the profiles of the individuals who use them. All Berliners enjoy equal access to education, irrespective of social position, age, gender, origin, religion, disability or sexual orientation. Berlin's educational providers are genuinely inclusive. Skills acquisition and lifelong learning are a matter of course in Berlin and readily accepted in the community. Each Berlin district has a wide range of private and public educational providers able to deliver low-threshold courses and react flexibly to the demands of the jobs market. This in turn benefits the Berlin jobs market by providing the necessary pool of skilled labour. The city is an attractive workplace for Berliners and, in particular, for skilled workers and executive personnel from the rest of Germany and abroad. Berlin has succeeded in meeting demand for skilled personnel both in the city and in its greater metropolitan region. Employers are also required to play their part by protecting and developing the pool of skilled workers and helping integrate into the jobs market those with fewer opportunities.

Source: www.stadtentwicklung.berlin.de/planen/stadtentwicklungskonzept/
download/strategie/BerlinStrategie_Broschuere_en.pdf, 2019

Union programmes, national-level investment through creative strategies and targeted policy goals, and through regional and local strategies. These levels of decision-making and investment tend to be focused on inclusion as well as priorities such as growth. Equally, the creative sector has – as noted earlier – been an umbrella for a very diverse range of activities. What does this mean conceptually? Returning to the central arguments made in Chapter 3, the national level has been somewhat unsuccessful in its attempts to foster behaviour change through nudge. In terms of the creative sector, there have been degrees of success through free entry to exhibitions for young people, for example. But the role of harnessing the creative sector through investment may not increase participation. Furthermore, the strategies set out in this chapter from the national and regional levels tend to be predicated on harnessing and developing existing areas of economic strength, such as the role of the creative sector in exports, digital, culture and heritage. Longer-term emphasis is placed on the development of training and investment in skills for the creative industries. On the other side of the creative coin, we have seen the importance of creative arts organisations in working with communities and driving forward aspects of economic development and renewal through the medium of the creative arts. These two aspects of the creative sector and its role in delivering economic development are both vital, and they seem to happily co-exist. So why should this matter? Practically, the engagement of communities in the

---

Box 5.4 Supranational context and funding

The creative and cultural industries is a term that includes a variety of different related industries. This definition includes not just 'cultural' industries but also 'creative' industries such as certain types of software work (e.g. new media and computer games). There has been considerable debate over the idea that the industries we suggest comprise the creative and cultural industries can in fact be aggregated. We agree that despite many similarities and interdependencies, the activities gathered under the umbrella of creative and cultural industries need also to be understood as separate industries in their own rights. The knowledge requirements, working methods, business and organisational models and consumer interfaces that define competitiveness in computer games are, for instance, very different to those that shape competitiveness in performance arts.

It is necessary to understand the creative and cultural industries not as a unified category but as an aggregate category. It is necessary to understand that the industries that make up the European creative and cultural industries' competitiveness share much but also exhibit unique and different cluster dynamics.

In particular Inner London and its surrounding regions and the Paris region figure prominently in most cases. However, despite the existence of prominent clusters in each of the industries many other centres exist.

Source: www.stadtentwicklung.berlin.de/planen/stadtentwicklungskonzept/
download/strategie/BerlinStrategie_Broschuere_en.pdf, 2019

creative arts has been an underpinning force for greater social cohesion and participation in the arts. These are important aspects of economic development and renewal. However, they tell us things about the way governance works that are theoretically vital. The success established with communities by creative arts like the Refugees' Kitchen (see Box 5.7) demonstrates success not only in driving participation in the creative arts but in engaging with wider social issues. This has meant that communities have adopted participatory behaviours, a shift in behaviour that has been difficult for top-down economic development initiatives to achieve (as noted in Chapter 3). What does this mean for the governance and institutional context set out earlier?

Furthermore, the roles of creative arts organisations in the creative sector disrupt established notions within governance theory that emphasise self-organisation, such as the role of governance networks. Such governance designs have regularly been posited as self-organising (Borzel, 1998, 2011), but have in reality tended to be driven by power relations that are the product of one or more competing institutional actors within the particular policy space. In this vein, the governance gap that creative arts groups have tended to fill (as discussed elsewhere in this chapter) is a product of the bargaining between governance actors within formal settings. The trust engendered between these organisations and community groups will be examined in terms of informal and formal dimensions of governance. Moreover, such formal or informal governance arrangements are typically mediated through established tiers of governance, networks or institutional levers or processes. These governance arrangements also take place amid a potential backdrop of collaborative tension. Confusion around communication, leadership, resources and power relations all frustrate the network process.

It seems apparent, therefore, that despite substantial investment in the creative sector as a drive for economic development, the barriers to engagement such as mistrust and complexities of governance delivery, or perceptions of a lack of consultation in previous economic development, the established conceptual governance approaches are unable to make sense of the roles of the community-facing creative arts organisations such as the Refugees' Kitchen (see Box 5.7). This is not a type of self-governance; it is merely de facto governance operating outside traditional governing and policy spaces. However, this is not a straightforward rupture between formal and informal governance. There are projects where creative arts groups seek to partner with educational institutions, local government, or access funding from these levels of governance such as the local level. However, these are deal-by-deal processes, rather than formal partnerships. Moreover, the roles of creative arts groups act as a disruption to established and accepted notions of governance and theory. In this vein, these groups disrupt the idea of self-governance, most often associated with Foucault. They are part of a wider governance map, but outside an

Box 5.5 Expansion of the creative sector

Maintaining and developing venues and premises for creative and cultural artists and businesses, a property policy safeguards and develops venues, assessing a range of occupancy claims with the help of a construction and planning law toolkit.

Facilitating the interim use of spaces

There are plans to set up a public–private space exchange to facilitate the interim use of open spaces and premises.

Improving the business skills of creative and cultural artists

Training and coaching help entrepreneurs from a range of backgrounds to establish themselves in the growing market.

Broadening participation in publicly funded cultural activities

Because culture is a form of education, local provision is safeguarded, inhibition levels are broken down, low-threshold venues are made available and networking and collaboration between organisations and the independent theatre scene are encouraged.

Supporting the spatial diversification of tourism demand

Increased tourism demand also benefits the outer city by transforming cultural venues into crystallisation points and catalysts for sensitive neighbourhood development.

Organising major events

In future more major national and international cultural and sporting events will be organised and used to develop infrastructure that will subsequently be available for both top-flight and grassroots use.

Source: www.stadtentwicklung.berlin.de/planen/stadtentwicklungskonzept/
download/strategie/BerlinStrategie_Broschuere_en.pdf

arena, not pushing to join this space. However, the ability of groups to self-govern is constrained by involvement in networks and partnerships in governance. Furthermore, there is a need to measure investment in social and economic development.

Conceptually, the enduring nature of New Public Management (NPM) is evident in these processes. From a governance perspective there is certainly a focus not only on targets and outcomes but also on efficient management processes and delivery. The enduring nature of NPM is not only evident in the reluctance to abandon goals of efficiency and effectiveness; it persists in the idea of targets as the first solution to which we turn in the fight against climate change, which is one of the most problematic conflicts of our era and for future eras. There are three aspects to this reticence of NPM, its stubbornness. First is the notion of measurement. Whether locally, nationally or globally, government responses to climate change questions are driven by the need to demonstrate improvement. This may be, some might suggest, for instrumental party political and electoral ends as well as to save the planet, but that is a question for another debate. The importance of measurement, and the ease of communicating measurement, continues to be the value of NPM. Measurement, in the context of policy responses to climate change, enables communication across problems, sectors and borders; should they wish, it enables governments to pressurise businesses to adopt measures towards carbon reduction, or lower emissions, or higher levels of recycling. Why these specific examples in the context of so many which relate to climate change? Because they can be measured and adopted – or enforced – across organisations which do not have borders, such as transnational corporations. The second enduring value of NPM lies in the related use of efficiency. Taking each of these aspects of NPM in turn, they possess value and suitability in underpinning responses to climate change as a policy problem. Next is targets and measurement. Across different varieties of NPM and in regard to climate change responses, the role of delivery is couched through targets (Shand, 2018).

The chapter now moves on to examine the question of governance partnerships and networks. The role of community-facing creative arts groups, that are seemingly able to connect with and develop lasting relationships with communities, creates an intriguing puzzle. Given the extent of supranational, national and regional attention devoted to capturing and growing the creative sector (such as the role of the Berlin 2030 strategy set out earlier in this chapter), the platform for communities to engage with the creative sector is firmly established. However, the success of groups such as Refugees' Kitchen in utilising the creative arts as a mechanism to drive this as a means of engaging communities and changing their behaviour to become involved in broader social and political issues raises questions. Is their success in this manner due to their existence outside the traditional governance arenas? The following sections examine the governance and institutional problems around this phenomenon.

Partnerships and networks

The overlapping and interlocking nature of the national-regional nature of governance in Germany in terms of delivery has been, across each of the national, regional and local tiers, one that has also embraced the role of networks or partnerships. In large-scale economic development programme, such as the Socially Integrative City, these delivery mechanisms were employed to harness the roles of varying public and private actors. These networks have been composed of various public, private and third sector across multi-levels. Such governance networks have been the subject of intense and long-standing debate in the scholarly literature, focused on ideas of network governance, partnership working (Borzel, 1998) or collaborative multi-agency delivery, and have led to approaches characterising the role of collaboration between the third sector and local government as the new public governance (Osborne, 2006, 2010). There is, in each of these approaches, a strong emphasis – and causal claims by scholars – on the role of power relations and tensions, as well as agency to organise among partners. These power dynamics evidently are then reflected in both the policy outcomes and funding decisions taken by these governance networks or delivery partnerships. Indeed, these mechanisms are set in existing institutional contexts, such as funding decisions for creative programmes by central government, external economic conditions or changes in political will that may affect these funds; changes to funding conditions at the supranational level; and are mediated through national governments in terms of distribution (Sorensen, 2013, 2012, 2006, 2002).

Informal governance

What is the role of community participation and engagement in this process?

It is tempting to position the roles of these community-facing creative arts groups as a kind of informal governance (Ayres, 2017). Certainly, their relationships and activities with community actors using the creative arts as means for changing behaviours to a more engaged and participatory role has been similar to that of a formal governance actor. Often, these groups are points of contact, advice centres and a means of support, as well as a way of accessing the creative arts. Informal governance tends to suggest activities within the formal arenas that are conducted by officials as part of everyday policy business (Ayres, 2017). Yet the relationships we see in creative arts group like the Refugees' Kitchen overtly use the arts as a means of addressing a political or social problem in the community, in this case, problems around social cohesion and community relations. Are these relationships then a kind of governance? The answer lies in the distinction between the formal and informal. As we saw in Chapter 3, formal governance mechanisms, typically at the national level, have experienced problems in trying to change or nudge behaviour. The top-down message, that individual agents need to live their lives differently, is often ignored or difficult to swallow. It is only harder regulation around behaviour change, such as advertising of cigarettes or gambling, that produces the change. However, though these are more extreme examples than the need to participate in the creative arts, we cannot ignore the success of community-facing groups

Box 5.6 Creative growth and direction

The number of companies has been growing continually since 2009. In 2015 the creative and cultural industries (CCI) sector numbered an estimated 250,600 companies. This is an increase of approximately 1.4 per cent over last year. The number of companies in the CCI sector has continually grown. These companies generated a turnover of EUR 150 billion in 2015. The projected increase is 2.4 per cent, another year of positive growth. The CCI sector contributed an estimated EUR 65.5 billion, about 2.2 per cent, to total gross value added in Germany in 2015. The number of employees subject to social insurance contributions went up once again, by 3.2 per cent to currently 834,300. If we also take into account the 250,600 self-employed persons in this sector, we arrive at a figure of approximately 1,085,000 core employees in the CCI sector. This corresponds to a growth-rate of more than 2.7 per cent over the last year.

The decrease in the number of marginally employed persons and concurrent increase in jobs with social insurance coverage is once again an indication that more individuals switched to regular jobs in the CCI sector in 2015. Assuming that there were approximately 349,000 marginally employed persons in 2014, this number dropped by almost 12 per cent to only 308,000 in 2015.

On the other hand, the number of marginally employed individuals, that is, self-employed persons and freelancers earning less than EUR 17,500 annually, remained stable at around 211,000. The overall number of people employed in this sector in 2015 was over 1.6 million. Due to the large decline in marginal employment, the overall number of people employed in 2015 was also lower than last year.

In 2015 the key indicators of the culture and creative industries improved once again in relation to the previous year, continuing the positive trend in the sector observed since 2009. However, numerous indicators show that the CCI economy is following the same trend as the overall economy. For example, the number of companies and the share of the CCI sector in the overall economy have remained nearly constant over the last years. The same applies to the percentage of gross value added, which has remained relatively constant over the past few years. Even though the number of employees subject to social insurance contributions increased significantly in past years, their share in the overall economy has increased only slightly.

Structurally, the culture and creative industries are traditionally dominated by a large number of small and micro enterprises. The average company in this sector employs 4.33 people, and on average 3.33 of them have jobs subject to social insurance contributions. Although the turnover per company has increased once again year on year (plus 1 per cent), the average turnover per CCI company – EUR 600,100 – remains relatively low compared to average company turnover in the overall economy. Viewing the CCI in Germany as a whole, each core employed person in the sector generates a turnover of EUR 138,600 and contributes EUR 60,300 to gross added value. The proportion of self-employed individuals in all core employed persons in the CCI economy fell slightly in recent years, and is presently at about 23 per cent.

Source: www.bmwi.de/Redaktion/EN/Publikationen/monitoring-of-selected-economic-key-data-on-culture-and-creative-industries-2016.pdf?__blob=publicationFile&v=4

to engage communities in participating in the arts, wider political life and in driving projects themselves. This in some contrast to the top-down nature of nudge-based policies that have come from central governments. Moreover, the success of these community-facing groups lies in the fact they are paced outside the formal established governance arenas, which are directed by formal rules of the game and institutional mechanisms. Informally, however, there are actors engaged in transformative work such as the creative arts community-facing groups in this book. The role of informal governance practices have tended to come about as a product of long-standing relationships at varying levels of formal governance mechanisms. Over time, these relationships and exchanges become nested: they are driven by long-established mutual trust and personal contacts. These ideas of informal governance, however, are not an answer in conceptually making sense of the self-organisation of anti-gentrification groups, for two main reasons. First, the informal nature of governance may reflect interactions and exchanges, but these take place within the formal nature of governance structures. Second, these are driven by personal connections, rather than the technological-driven agent-based exchange and interaction we see in the self-organisation of anti-gentrification groups.

Governance theory

Reframing the theory: the role of the creative sector in terms of institutions, governance and behaviour

Challenges to participation in economic development initiative are also present in the complexities of governance bodies and decision-making and of wider governance (Ayres, 2017) in working with communities and in driving economic development programmes more generally. In order to be workable and enduring mechanisms, however, governance and delivery processes that will overcome existing challenges to participation must underpin economic development programmes, therefore, engaging with communities to drive participation and behaviour change is vital in terms of participation in creative arts and wider development and urban renewal programmes. These tend to be, as noted elsewhere in this book, that there is a mistrust of information from government and that individuals feel they are being compromised in making their own decisions (John, 2017). This is key to achieving more long-lasting behaviour change and greater levels of trust in the community, leading to shifts in practice among resident communities. Behaviour change from the national level through public policy has met with mixed results. The challenge of changing behaviours or to embed nudges in public policy, such as to drive increased participation in the arts, is a grand challenge. The role of behaviour in urban renewal is important, as development often entails physical and social change. However, the examples in the chapter of community engagement demonstrate the value of bottom-up working with communities that has enabled aspects of development and engagement. This avoids the problems of mistrust that have been problematic for behavioural public policy. There is huge potential for mistrust in nudge-based public policies that are embedded in economic development initiatives that suggest new homes, transient communities, changes in economic life and leisure time, emphasis on changes in the social aspects of life such as the arts and education, are also significant. This is driven by problems such as rapid and visible change, top-down decision-making and a feeling of a lack of consultation within communities.

Moreover, there can be issues in urban renewal and development projects to place too great an emphasis on the complexities of governance and decision-making, that frustrates the relationship with the community. In understanding the role of agents in governance processes, the institutional role is one that constrains and shapes the abilities of the agent. The agent, however, outside of the institutional sphere and formal governing arena, is seen as not able to shape their way without recourse to institutional processes. For example, the creative arts groups obey local and national laws; they are subject to regulation; they bid for funding from varying tiers of governance. However, they operate outside these formal processes:

> In an attempt to comprehend the relationship between agency and structure Giddens (1976) considered that social structures incorporate material and symbolic parts. For Giddens social structure is the product of human action (agency). Agency involves a 'stream of actual or contemplated causal interventions of corporeal beings in the ongoing process of events in the world' (Giddens 1976, 75). Agents are socialised in institutions through an evolving set of roles and relationship. Agency and the social domain develop together through an interactive and iterative process. Agents accommodate their roles and relationships in the context of their positions in the institution; agents internalise roles, relationships and expectations that allow them to function in a specific situation. Giddens considers that structuration describes how the agent is produced by the structure, which incorporates the objectification of past actions by agents. Giddens uses purposiveness and intentionality in a phenomenological context when explaining his notion of structuration and the rationalisation of agency. 'Rationalization is the causal expression of the grounding of

the purposiveness of the agent in self-knowledge and in the knowledge of the social and material worlds which are the environment of the acting self' (Giddens 1976, 85). In addition, Bourdieu (1977, 1990) used phenomenological dialectic procedures to explain relationships between agents and structures through 'externalisation of the internal', and 'internalisation of the external'. Through the notion of 'habitus' individual agents develop perceptions, perspectives or 'system of dispositions' through objective conditions encountered in the world. Objective social structures are absorbed into the subjective mental experience of agents; the objective external world imposes requirements on agents which require internalisation if institutional membership and/or acceptance is to be realised. Objective social structures are internalised into personal cognitive perspectives so the subjective activity of the agent becomes commensurate with the objective structures. Both Giddens and Bourdieu recognise the relationships between individual agents and institutional structures and provide an assessment of the relationship between them. In this study we examine this relationship through the development of an evolving institution and the extent wider societal ideas, 'systems of dispositions' through leadership provide the basis for path-dependency and cultural transformation. Institutions only change in relation to past decisions; change is 'path-dependent in that initial choices determine later developments and once a particular pathway is selected, alternatives tend to be ruled out thereafter' (Bulmer and Burch 2001, 81).

(Howell and Shand, 2015: 508)

Partnerships and the New Public Governance: communities and governance design

The role of overlapping tiers of governance in the German case is evident through the funding streams across the creative sector, especially through policy strategies such as Berlin 2030. However, the complexities of governance delivery can frustrate attempts to engage communities in civic life and the political process (Sorensen, 2014). Through working with communities, creative arts organisations have successfully engaged in behaviour change in ways that top-down initiatives have thus far failed to do. This is not driven by a formal partnership arrangement or through working with established third-sector organisations. The long-established roles of groups that have campaigned against the outcomes of economic development as a neo-liberal agenda also set the context of bottom-up groups against the established governance structures. While creative arts groups such as the Refugees' Kitchen (see Box 5.7) are vital in visible campaigns, their role as de facto governance points of contact are essential in communities' engagement. These established modes of governance delivery have been tended to be driven by multiple actors in a pluralistic state that is configured through networks and partnerships, often with third-sector partners. However, this process of establishing partnership, we can argue, draws the partner from the campaigning realm into the formal governing arena. What is different about groups such as bottom-up organisations like the Refugees' Kitchen, is that they remain outside the formal governing and institutional arenas. This structure–agency underpinning in governance delivery has seen, however, creative arts groups remaining outside the formal decision-making arenas, and out with models of delivery such as governance networks and a messy governance process. Changes to governance delivery have not produced inter-organisational working and focused delivery, rather they have left aspects of provision in the creative sector where community-facing groups have moved in and acted as de facto officials, with their remit of participation and activity in the creative arts arena broadened to include aspects of wider political and civic life. This also means a greater likelihood of mistrust in top-down institutional approaches and formal governance initiatives. However, the community in German governance processes has held an important role in recent large-scale economic development programmes:

> Community groups in the Social City (and in Germany more generally) have an advantage over their British counterparts. A respondent from the Greens noted that communities in Germany have been awarded legal rights regarding self government and related to planning decisions ... The fact that community actors could choose in effect which efforts to finance made the Social City initially hard to govern. This problem for the Social City will be realised as the issues that the programme seeks to address are unlikely to be resolved by the renewal initiative. In Potsdam the role of community actors and the question of Quartiersmanagement have to be considered alongside the role of those private patrons who individually fund the restoration projects of museums and historic attractions in the region.
>
> (Shand, 2013: 5–6)

Legitimacy

The elected levels of governance have invested in the creative sector across national, regional and local levels. Moreover, there has been substantial investment in the creative sector in Germany through EU-funded programmes, such as Horizon 2020 and the European Regional Development Fund (ERDF). The German context for the creative sector has a policy history of both success and tension. The success of the creative sector in large cities such as Berlin and Hamburg has been a driver for job creation and growth, and broader policy goals such as increased tourism. The role of culture in driving the visitor economy has been vital in the Berlin case. More broadly, the levels of funding have driven projects around participation education, skills and training. The role of legitimacy is especially important in the German context, as the history of the creative sector in Germany has resulted in successful economic development but also a reaction from creative arts campaigners and groups that oppose these changes, especially in terms of housing, and the effect on changes to communities through gentrification. This consequence of economic development and renewal has meant there is a long-standing tension in German governance between economic development initiatives and creative arts as a means of protest. Though to some critics of economic development programmes, this may question the legitimacy of governing institutions, there is a broader question of legitimacy. The creative arts organisations such as the Refugees' Kitchen (see Box 5.7) have occupied a type of governance space that has reached communities and engaged them in broader social issues through the creative arts.

The roles of the differing levels of governance (supranational, national, regional and local) and their investments in the creative sector and the creative arts more broadly from central government has a range of effects in terms of the creative sector and its role as a driver for renewal and economic development. First, the longer-term focus on the creative sector as a mechanism for developing jobs, skills and growth shows the means of the creative sector to address long-standing social issues such as unemployment, and the need for funding in the creative and cultural industries areas to reward existing and established areas of growth.

In engaging communities in the creative arts, the scope of these bottom-up organisations has a long history in Germany, and is also a current tension in German economic development. The effects of gentrification in Berlin have been seen as a negative consequence of economic development and urban renewal in the housing sector. The tensions these kinds of developments have led to demonstrate the role of the creative sector in bottom-up community politics in the housing arena. What of creative arts organisations, however, which have a broader agenda of renewal and social reform?

Does this take place in a formal or informal manner?

As unelected organisations, these agendas are set outside the governance and institutional walls. However, the goals of these organisations and the community-focused activity demonstrated by projects like Refugees' Kitchen show there is a type of legitimacy bestowed by the community on these actors. Though this is an informal type of legitimacy, it is one driven by the existence of creative arts organisations outside traditional established governing and institutional structures. This trust in fostering grassroots participation from communities has given a kind of legitimacy to the creative arts organisations, in two main ways. First, this has been driven by the trust engendered in these actors through community participation.

Second, the role of these actors outside the established structures has also facilitated their role as a point of contact for the community. The gap between formal legitimacy and informal legitimacy is different from that of a charity, for example. Though the lens of the creative arts has been the driving force behind this engagement, this has opened up a much broader role in terms of the community. Indeed, several social aspects of renewal and urban development are key concerns of Refugees' Kitchen. The role of creative arts as a participatory doorway into wider aspects of economic development and renewal is key, and the success of these goals by organisations such as the Refugees' Kitchen relies on sustained participation in these initiatives. This differs from the notion of Arnstein's ladder of participation (1969) in that some communities have found barriers to participation through factors such as complexities of governance structures and lack of social capital. The behaviour change in participation through grassroots organisations has shown participation, but the underpinning engagement has not taken place through formal channels with established governance institutions.

Governmentality

The discourse around creative economy and the role of the creative arts in economic development more broadly has been one of participation and legacy. The governmentality of the creative sector in the German context is characterised by overlapping tiers. This delivery model shows these overlapping competencies and the importance of the creative sector in driving economic development and renewal in cities. The importance therefore of the varying tiers of governance – the local, the regional and the national – are key in delivery. As noted elsewhere in this book, the complexities of governance systems – such as networks – can be a negative force in engaging communities in civic life. The complexities of governance systems and the resultant disaffection among communities are evident in the protests around what some groups see as the negative consequences of economic development, such as gentrification.

Co-production

The German context is different in terms of governance partnerships, as often these are overlapping competencies in delivery. The roles of co-creative or co-productive mechanisms have been driven in some contexts by austerity and the need to maintain already constrained services. However, in the context of overlapping governance, delivery between the national and regional levels demonstrates the enduring problem of gaps in governance engagement. The role of partnership has been highlighted by creative arts organisations in engaging with communities and local authorities. However, this does not lead to a process of transition of these organisations moving into the established formal governance and institutional arenas. It is the very informality of the relationship that has fostered the trust resulting in participation and behaviour change among these local communities.

The multi-level nature of governance mechanisms in the German context has seen aspects of the creative sector driven through partnerships in some respects – for example, the funding streams and programmes examined earlier in the chapter, such as EU-level funds. The roles of these partnerships between multiple levels of actors or between creative arts groups and communities are a significant mode of governance delivery in the creative sector. However, this has also been a highly innovatory tool of public service design and delivery, and the need for grassroots community engagement and participation is equally pressing. To be sure, these priorities overlap; so it is striking that the creative sector should produce two such different sides of what is in effect the same creative coin. The top-down nature of governance drives economic development through the means of the creative sector by focusing on investment and growth as public policy priorities from national-level governments. Meanwhile, in parallel, the bottom-up role of community-facing creative arts organisations achieves greater participation and engagement with political and civic life through the lens of the creative arts. Each of these processes takes place at the same time, towards overlapping goals of the creative sector as a means of driving economic development (such as participation, community development, and education and skills development). Yet these top-down and bottom-up processes appear to occur independently of one another.

But why should this matter? If, for example, these two sides of the creative sector coin happily co-exist and drive economic development in different

---

Box 5.7 Refugees' Kitchen

Refugees' Kitchen is a mobile kitchen, created by artists and refugees in collaboration. It rolls from city to city and illuminates the respective region from which the refugee seekers have fled – culinary and with additional programmes: concerts, lectures, discussions, etc.

At various inner-city locations, refugees from each region cook traditional food in the Refugees' Kitchen. Political information about the food is also provided in small snacks: background information on wars and crises, government systems, military interventions, history of the respective country. Fast food with fast facts on crisis areas.

Refugees' Kitchen underpins the subject of flight with subjective stories as well as with political backgrounds, and confronts (world) politically uninterested people with the topic of flight.

Source: http://refugeeskitchen.de/

ways, this is not an issue. However, conceptually, this is an important point to unpack. The role of trust has been an obstacle in terms of participation in governance and in changing behaviour. The complexities of existing governance mechanisms also may negatively impose themselves on individuals who are deterred from engaging in civic life. The roles of creative arts organisations, which often have broad goals in terms of economic development and social change, are examined in the following sections.

Filling in a governance gap?

The disruptions to established governance theory through examining these creative sector contexts demonstrate two distinct halves of the creative sector in the economic development arena: the top-down institutional policy priorities in developing the creative sector and economic activity in these areas; and the more bottom-up creative arts organisations that challenge these policy priorities. The German context – especially in Berlin – has been one where these tensions around urban renewal and economic development have resulted in protests and campaigns. These have focused on problems of gentrification and the changing physical aspect of urban areas as a result of investment in the creative economy, especially with regard to housing. The unintended consequences of economic development and renewal projects in urban areas has led to negative outcomes for some communities such as gentrification, rising house prices and problems with social cohesion.

These problems in achieving renewal and economic development outcomes have prompted bottom-up creative arts groups to target renewal through the creative arts. While this may seem vastly different from the top-down policy priorities in the creative sector at the national and regional levels, both top-down policy goals and bottom-up creative arts organisations have similar and overlapping aims. These include increased social cohesion, community engagement, job creation and business growth. So why should we think about the notion of a governance gap? First, despite the broad definition of the creative sector, there are clear gaps in achieving economic development through creativity. These investments in the broader creative sector across this broad range of activities, such as digital development, gaming and exports, have enormous potential to deliver economic development and renewal. However, there are aspects of renewal and development that are not captured within the top-down nature of the creative sector. These aspects of development and renewal – such as community participation in the creative sector – are driven by creative arts organisations.

Practically and conceptually, the accessibility of Refugees' Kitchen demonstrates a bottom-up renewal project outside the established institutional arenas. As discussed in the theoretical sections earlier in this chapter, there is a tension between the top-down investment in the creative sector and the bottom-up community-focused creative arts projects. Both of these sides of the debate, in different ways, foster economic development and renewal. The core policy focuses at the national and regional levels emphasise employment, skills and training, as well as diverse aims in growth from digital technologies to exports. Governance is reframed in these contexts. Though both sides of the sector co-exist, and are drivers for development and renewal, the de facto roles of governance taken on by community arts organisations go beyond ideas of informal governance. This is distinct from the informal governance undertaken by established institutional and governing mechanisms that shadows the everyday business of formal governance within governing and regulatory arenas. Rather, the schisms we see in the creative sector in the German context demonstrate the de facto governance roles taken on by organisations and projects such as Refugees' Kitchen. Conceptually, as discussed, these events present ruptures to existing ideas of governance, behaviour and institutional roles. Creative arts organisations are occupying these policy spaces and providing mechanisms – such as the Refugees' Kitchen project – to achieve aspects of economic development and renewal. In this vein, these organisations are filling a governance gap for these communities, not just through participation, but as a visible point of contact. Furthermore, the role of these organisations differs from established notions of partnership working in governance. As discussed earlier in this chapter, ideas of partnership governance that emphasise collaboration between the third sector and local or regional levels differ from the example of creative arts organisations. There are also disruptions to ideas of behavioural public policy. As examined earlier in this chapter and at length in Chapter 3, nudge-based policies have failed to deliver the anticipated benefits in policy spaces such as the environment or health. The role of nudge plus in attempting to drive behaviour change from a bottom-up perspective and avoid issues of the top-down nature of behaviour-based public policy is also different to the behaviour change demonstrated in communities that has been driven by creative arts organisations like Refugees' Kitchen. The bottom-up nature of these organisations avoids the issues of perceptions of misinformation and mistrust that have dogged attempts at behaviour change from national governments.

Concluding remarks

This chapter has examined the role of the creative sector in economic development in Germany. The initial sections of the chapter explored the national level's policy priorities in investing across a broad range of creative industries. The discussion then critically examined the success of Berlin in the creative sector, and moved on to focus on the roles of bottom-up creative arts organisations. This discussion has particularly focused on the anti-gentrification debate and the use of creative arts in these protests. In addressing the conceptual importance of these tensions, the chapter then moved on to examine the disruptions to governance theory and institutional thought that have arisen from these tensions in the creative sector.

The diverse range of creative activities characterised as policy priorities in the German context is not at the expense of investment. The drive to foster greater innovation in areas of existing strength and the need to use these as drivers for economic development and renewal, however, have been the very cause of ruptures in the governance process. The bottom-up creative arts organisations that act as drivers for economic development and renewal initiatives have focused on community-driven work, and an organic approach to renewal. The example of Refugees' Kitchen demonstrates the role of the creative arts in driving urban renewal through social engagement, community cohesion and participation in the creative arts. The cultural impact of the kitchen, founded and driven by artists, has achieved several economic development and renewal goals – chiefly, that of increased social cohesion and widening participation in the creative arts.

The core findings of the German case study, focused on Berlin, show the creative sector characterised as a broad range of creative and cultural activities. These industries are drawn from the crafts and heritage industries, tourism, digital medias and gaming, and more traditional classical forms of the creative arts. The policy strategies nationally, regionally and locally focus on the need to invest in areas that will engender growth and create more jobs and develop skills. However, policy agendas such as Berlin 2030 also focus on the importance of integrating the creative sector with aspects of economic development and renewal like green space and the green economy.

The importance of creative arts organisations like Refugees' Kitchen in Germany in engaging communities and using the lens of the creative arts to address wider social issues is vital in engendering behaviour change towards greater participation in the creative arts, but also, even more crucially perhaps, in wider social issues that affect economic development and renewal. The conceptual consequences of this relationship, as discussed in this chapter, are important in understanding the ways in which governance institutions engage with communities and the creative sector; how short- and long-term success in economic development can be achieved; and the ways in which funding is allocated across different levels of governance. The next chapter moves on to examine the creative sector and economic development in the Canadian context, focusing on the themes of funding, governance and institutions, and communities. The chapter then moves on to address the meaning for governance theory and the roles of community groups across the creative arts.

References

Arnstein, S. (1969) A ladder of citizen participation *Journal of the American Institute of Planners* 35 (4): 216–224

Ayres, S. (2017) Assessing the impact of informal governance on political innovation *Public Management Review* 19 (1): 90–107

Bader, B. and Bialluch, M. (2009) Gentrification and the creative class in Berlin-Kreuzberg. In: Porter, L. and Shaw, K. (eds) *Whose urban renaissance? An international comparison of urban regeneration strategies* Abingdon: Routledge

Borzel, T. (1998) Organising Babylon: On the different conceptions of policy networks *Public Administration* 76 (2): 253–273

Borzel, T. (2011) Networks: Reified metaphor or governance panacea? *Public Administration* 89 (1): 49–63

Bourdieu, P. (1977) *Outline of a theory of practice* London: Cambridge University Press

Bourdieu, P. (1990) *The logic of practice* Cambridge: Polity Press.

Darras, B. (2019) Creativity and creative communities. In: *The international encyclopedia of art and design* London and New York: Wiley

Guthmann Estate (2019) Real estate report Berlin https://guthmann.estate/en/market-report/

Herrigel, G. (2010) *Manufacturing possibilities: Creative action and industrial recomposition in the United States, Germany, and Japan* Oxford: Oxford University Press

Howell, K. E. and Shand, R. (2015) Welsh devolution and leadership: Power, discourse and identity *Policy Studies* 36 (5): 507–521

John, P. (2017) *How far to nudge? Assessing behavioural public policy* Cheltenham: Edward Elgar

Kil, W. and Silver, H. (2006) From Kreuzberg to Marzahn: New migrant communities in Berlin *German Politics and Society* 24 (4): 95–121

McRobbie, A. (2011) Re-thinking creative economy as radical social enterprise *Variant* 41: 32–33

Mossig, I. (2011) Regional employment growth in the cultural and creative industries in Germany 2003–2008 *European Planning Studies* 19 (6): 967–990

Nathan, M., Pratt, A and Rincon-Aznar, A. (2015) *Creative economy employment in the EU and the UK* NESTA

Osborne, S. (2006) The new public governance? *Public Management Review* 8 (3): 377–387

Osborne, S. (2010) *The new public governance: Emerging perspectives on the theory and practice of public governance* Abingdon: Routledge

Park, W. and Hong, P. (2019) *Innovator companies in Germany: Creative innovative firms from Japan* New York: Springer

Power, D. (2011) Priority sector report: Creative and cultural industries *Innova Report* No. 16: European Commission

Radomska, J., Wołczek, P., Sołoducho-Pelc, L. and Silva, S. (2019) The impact of trust on the approach to management – a case study of creative industries *Sustainability* 11 (3): 816

Schmidt, V. (2001) Federalism and state governance in the EU and the U.S.: An institutional perspective. In: Nicolaides, K. and Howse, R. (eds) *The federal vision* Oxford: Oxford University Press

Shafi, M., Yang, Y., Khan, Z. and Yu, A. (2019) Vertical co-operation in creative micro-enterprises: A case study of textile crafts of Matiari District, Pakistan *Sustainability* 11 (3): 920

Shand, R. (2013) *Governing sustainable urban renewal: Partnerships in action* Abingdon: Routledge

Shand, R. (2018) The role of ethics and targets in environmental governance and the enduring importance of new public management *Political Studies Review* 16 (3): 230–239

Sorensen, E. (2002) Democratic theory and network governance *Administrative Theory & Praxis* 24 (4): 693–720

Sorensen, E. (2006) Metagovernance: The changing role of politicians in processes of democratic governance *American Review of Public Administration* 36 (1): 98–114

Sorensen, E. (2012) Governance networks as a frame for inter-demoi participation and deliberation *Administrative Theory & Praxis* 34 (4): 509–532

Sorensen, E. (2013) Institutionalizing interactive governance for democracy *Critical Policy Studies* 7 (1): 72–86

Sorensen, E. (2014) The metagovernance of public innovation in governance networks *Policy & Politics* conference in Bristol, 16–17 September 2014

UNESCO (2012) https://en.unesco.org/creativity/sites/creativity/files/periodic_report/Germany_exsummary_EN_2012.pdf

Wedemeier, J. (2010) The impact of the creative sector on growth in German regions *European Planning Studies* 18 (4): 505–520

Wiesand, A. and Soendermann, M. (2005) *The 'creative sector': An engine for diversity, growth, and jobs in Europe* Amsterdam: European Cultural Foundation

Wyszomirski, M. (2004) *Defining and developing creative sector initiatives* Ohio: Ohio University Press

6 Canada

The Creative Inter Cities Network to Artscape

This chapter examines our third case study, that of the Creative Inter Cities Network in Canada. The key themes of this initiative emphasise many of the debates already discussed in the book, such as the urban-rural divide, squaring the circle of investment and innovation, and community engagement. The chapter proceeds as follows. First, we will focus on the core projects and aims of the Creative Inter Cities Network, before moving on to unpack the key progress on projects. The chapter then moves on to focus on the patterns of investment, spending and the modes of behaviour in the creative initiative, such as behaviour change, nudge and impacts of the creative network in terms of economic development. The chapter finally moves on to the learning for governance modes and delivery in the case study from these nudges and behaviours, and examines how established governance, institutional and behavioural theory can be reframed by the findings here.

Funding and delivery in the creative sector

The nature of governance in the creative sector in Germany is driven by three different levels of both governance and delivery. The funding programmes, which will be interrogated later on in this chapter in detail, focus on skills development and training, as well as embedding creativity at the heart of renewal and development. The national, regional and local levels each focus on the role of creativity in driving job creation, physical place-making and linkage to education, green space, tourism and cultural development (Canadian Heritage, 2018). Table 6.1 sets out the key policy priorities and the core funders.

Linkage to broader economic development and renewal

How does the creative sector align with the broader policy goals of economic development and renewal? Nationally, there has been a recent focus on the need to emphasise social cohesion, housing, education, sustainability and diversity. In addition, there is a clear focus on drawing upon

Table 6.1 Political economy of the creative sector in Canada

Project	Funders	Level of governance	Key partners	Political era
Creative Canada Policy Framework	National Government	National; regional	CBC – Radio Canada	2017–
Canada Book Fund	National Government	National; regional	Department of Canadian Heritage, Canada Council for the Arts, Telefilm Canada, Canadian Radio-television and Telecommunications Commission, Canadian Broadcasting Corporation, National Film Board of Canada, National Arts Centre, National Gallery of Canada	2012–
Canada Arts Presentation Fund	National Government	National; regional	Department of Canadian Heritage, Canada Council for the Arts, Telefilm Canada, Canadian Radio-television and Telecommunications Commission, Canadian Broadcasting Corporation, National Film Board of Canada, National Arts Centre, National Gallery of Canada	2012–

Source: www.canada.ca/en/canadian-heritage/campaigns/creative-canada/framework/at-a-glance.html; https://en.unesco.org/creativity/policy-monitoring-platform/government-canada-cultural, 2020.

strengths such as tourism, history and business development. Recent large-scale economic development and renewal initiatives nationally in Canada such as the Creative Cities Network have drawn upon the importance of heritage and crafts as much as they have emphasised the need to create jobs and training programmes. These focuses are also reflected in the national and regional levels of governance and funding. A UNESCO study found that these priorities were demonstrated across policy goals for the creative sector in different areas. For example, the commonalities across different municipalities reflect national priorities but also include local variations that enable growth and development of the creative sector. UNESCO research found that there was distinct focus on both heritage and growth (UNESCO, 2014: 5):

> Measures implemented by provincial and territorial organizations are numerous and cover all the stages of cultural expression. A short sample of four examples is provided below. From 2007 to 2010, British Columbia's Arts Partners in Creative Development (APCD) invested more than CA$6 million in 84 projects in 16 BC communities. APCD was a strategic investment partnership assisting the province's organizations in creating and developing new works with the intent of producing or exhibiting them at the highest standard. Through its investments, APCD facilitated the creation of new work to showcase both locally and worldwide. Organizations were funded to create, commission and develop original work in the performing, visual, media and literary arts. The Cultural Opportunities for Youth Program was created by the Government of Nova Scotia in 2007 to promote artistic development and community cultural development. The program supports special or pilot projects that foster artistic skills development for youth, foster audience development, and contribute to knowledge and experience in the community. The New Brunswick Book Policy, titled 'Creating a Culture of Books and Reading', was launched in September 2009. This Policy outlines the government's objectives and strategies to strengthen the publishing industry, to increase access to New Brunswick books, and to promote and foster reading. The book policy outlines six objectives with specific strategies to be addressed in the three-year action plan. Finally, Culture On The Go is a pilot program that supports greater access for Saskatchewan artists and cultural products through touring and marketing opportunities. It is a research-focused, application-driven and peer-adjudicated pilot program that tests new and innovative ideas to deliver funding to touring Saskatchewan artists, Saskatchewan presenters, and 'run-out' performances by artists (i.e. no overnight stays). The CA$800,000 pilot program is administered by the Saskatchewan Arts Board. A Touring Advisory Panel has been be formed to make sure that the program complements existing touring programs. Preference is given

to project proposals that incorporate the following seven elements: a spectrum of engagement from emerging to professional; youth engagement; access; Saskatchewan content; Aboriginal content; community legacy; and new media.

The role of the federal and national levels in driving the creative sector forward is vital in unpacking the governance processes around the creative sector in the Canadian context. The following sections of the chapter now move on to focus on the governance and institutional context for the creative sector in economic development in Canada. The key aspects of the role of the creative sector in driving economic development are covered, focused on the political economy of these projects. The key funders and power relations, and the differing political perspectives that affect the creative sector, are also examined.

Governance and institutional context in Canada

The governance and institutional context for the creative economy and creative arts more broadly in Canada focuses on the national level of funding and policy priorities around the creative economy and creative arts. The Creative City Network of Canada as an empirical focus of this chapter is set within the context of core policy priorities and underpinning principles of funding direction. This wider policy focus around participation, engagement and communities is supported by strategic national funds targeted to certain states. At the regional and national levels, participation is traced year-by-year.

In terms of funding, the key actors driving the creative sector in Canada are drawn from the public and private sectors, and are multi-levelled in nature. In the first instance, there is a large amount of investment across the broad church of the creative sector in Canada by the national level. However, there is significant investment and delivery of creative arts programmes by states at the municipal level. These programmes tend to be driven by education and training, business development and growth, and the need to bridge the urban-rural divide.

Disruptions to established debates

Established debates have focused on the role of bottom-up groups, often driven by campaigns around funding for the arts, community politics and the broader creative economy. Here we can see a clear distinction between these two areas (as discussed at length in Chapter 2). The funding priorities and underpinning policy focus represent a clear governmental drive to invest in the creative industries, and in providing elevation for areas of creativity that are already performing well. However, the debates around innovation in the creative sector are well established (Jaaniste, 2009;

Wyszomirski, 2004; Volkerling, 2001), and the debates have also focused on the role of non-productivity in Canada (Leger, 2010); the role of creative cities and innovation; and the problems of workplace equity and equality (Shade and Jacobson, 2015) as well as the role of precarity in work in the creative economy (Murray and Gollmitzer, 2012). The linkage to wider societal change and the benefits of the creative economy are also documented by Stern and Seifert (2008), and in the context of communications and connectivity (Stolarick *et al.*, 2005). Equally, the creative sector has important overlapping tendencies with the green economy and sustainability more broadly (Suciu and Nasulea, 2019), and as an important driver for future education and training in Canada (Harris and de Bruin, 2019). Moreover, the reach of the creative sector in the Canadian context has been examined in debates from the role of scientific production and trade policy for the creative sector (Jacobi, 2019). These debates in the literature demonstrate the large scope – and vast scale – of the creative sector. These debates, while addressing aspects of economic development and renewal, such as education or growth, have not focused on the overarching landscape of the creative sector in terms of economic development and renewal. The importance of the creative sector in Canada in driving economic development and renewal is detailed through both national and municipal policy goals. These are a broad range of priorities, such as heritage, investment in skills and job creation, gaming, digital and the arts. There are a number of national-level drivers to increase the role of the creative sector through investment and developing the skills and learning base to foster longer-term job creation and growth across the creative sector. There are also a number of bottom-up creative arts organisations that engage communities in the creative arts and not only seek to drive participation in creative arts projects locally, but to engender a broader behaviour change in terms of communities. This will be examined in the latter stages of this chapter. The chapter now moves on to focus on the role of national-level policy goals and investment priorities in the creative sector in Canada.

What are the key organisations that drive the creative sector and what are the implications for economic development and governance?

The Creative City Network of Canada

What are the key policy priorities for the creative sector?

The Creative City Network of Canada (CCNC) has produced a comprehensive report detailing the institutional capacity that supports the creative arts and industries. Through detailing the economic importance and longer-term impacts of the creative arts and industries in rural areas, the report also focuses to a large extent on the importance of underpinning creative industries in their development and economic vitality in driving rural economic development. To this end, evidently the geographic scale of Canada is a challenge for the CCNC in achieving creative economic development. In terms of unpacking these challenges, the differing cultural heritages and traditions that underpin the initiative are chiefly those of funding and modes of governance. The importance of creative economic development in rural areas is underlined by long-established social issues such as 'declining and ageing populations, youth retention, limited economic and social opportunities, depleting natural resources, loss of local services, and higher costs of living' (Hill, 2012). These challenges are not just those of job creation, skills development or greater connectivity. They are also more profoundly rooted in the need to connect communities to the creative arts, public life and to harness existing skills in these areas.

The pace of change and creative economic development

The emphasis on visible change in economic development initiatives and related shifts in behaviour also pose temporal questions. The pace of change, if gauged wrongly, can mean disruptions to

> the ways the community understands, celebrates, and expresses itself. And these are major contributing factors to its ability to withstand the economic, political, and cultural winds of change. Arts, culture, and heritage are not only amenities to improve quality of life, but are a foundation upon which the future of rural and small communities rests. Arts and creative activities can profoundly affect the ability of a town not only to survive over time, but to thrive.
>
> (Hill, 2012)

The ownership of ideas that drive creative arts projects and related economic development initiatives is vital in working towards economic development. The role of the community as embedded in the process rather than simply receiving ideas, goals or funding is crucial in achieving sustainable economic development that can be embedded within communities. The Creative City seeks to draw upon the changing nature of the creative arts:

> The role of the arts in rural communities have diversified and are increasingly coupled with ideas of 'creative economy' opportunities. For example, typical arts-involved projects for youth engagement highlight building social connections, self-esteem, and community knowledge. While such social and community-focused aspects of meaningful cultural engagement are crucial, emerging initiatives indicate that these traditional views on the contributions of arts activities

are broadening to include ideas about cultural/creative employment and enterprises ... The two perspectives of community cultural development (emphasising social roles) and economic development (from the economic impacts of festivals to attracting and fostering creative businesses) are equally important and, in fact, are interdependent. The growing recognition of artists, creators, and entrepreneurial creative individuals as potential residents and business owners in rural areas seeking to diversify their economic base offers a widening path to re-think the contribution of arts and creative activities to these communities.

(Hill, 2012)

Governance and institutions

What is the role of creative arts organisations in economic development?

The focus of the Creative Inter Cities Network (CICN) is on top-down funding and stimulus for the creative economy, across traditional cleavages such as urban and rural, or socio-economic barriers to participation and success.

Box 6.1 Funding and investment

- Starting in 2018, increase federal funding to the Canada Media Fund to directly support jobs for Canadian writers, producers, directors, actors and technical crews.
- Collaborate with Innovation, Science and Economic Development Canada (ISED) on implementing the plan to conduct the review of both the Broadcasting Act and the Telecommunications Act, as announced in Budget 2017.
- Collaborate with ISED on supporting the Parliamentary Review of the Copyright Act.
- Begin delivering the investment of an additional C$300 million over ten years in arts and heritage infrastructure through the Canada Cultural Spaces Fund. Part of this funding will be to construct, renovate and equip creative hubs that bring artists, cultural entrepreneurs and organisations together that build entrepreneurial skills, create, collaborate and innovate, and help generate new markets for Canadian creativity.

Experimentation project: Canada Arts Presentation Fund will be temporarily suspending the formal incorporation requirement for applicants from Indigenous and ethnocultural groups in 2018–2019, to see if removing this perceived barrier leads to an increase in funded projects among these populations.

Source: www.canada.ca/content/dam/pch/documents/campaigns/
creative-canada/CCCadreFramework-EN.pdf

The importance of central funding and focus on the creative arts and the creative economy more instrumentally leads us to revisit aspects of governance theory. For example, the emphasis on the role of participation across creative arts projects could be viewed as a type of nudge. The importance of institutional processes in governance, however, is key in unpacking the role of theory. As we discussed at length in Chapter 3, the role of the creative arts is one that has sat outside institutional walls, and has been driven by bottom-up organisations or community-focused initiatives. However, the question of central government funding raises questions as to the extent and reach of the state in the creative arts and their role in renewal and development. The central focus of funding from central government demonstrates commitments through varying types of industrial strategy to grow the creative arts and the creative economy. However, the focus of this funding also targets less affluent areas and regions in attempts to drive the growth of the creative sector as a mechanism for increased skills development and employment. However, there are important questions here about economic development and renewal. Does this investment from national- and regional-level governance tiers result in greater participation and engagement in the creative sector from communities, and how is the sector conceptualised?

Box 6.2 Governance and strategy

Internal Services are those groups of related activities and resources that the federal government considers to be services in support of programs and/or required to meet corporate obligations of an organization. Internal Services refers to the activities and resources of the 10 distinct service categories that support Program delivery in the organization, regardless of the Internal Services delivery model in a department. The 10 service categories are: Management and Oversight Services; Communications Services; Legal Services; Human Resources Management Services; Financial Management Services; Information Management Services; Information Technology Services; Real Property Services; Materiel Services; and Acquisition Services.

Planning highlights
The Prime Minister expects all Ministers to:

- Commit to an open, honest government that is accountable to Canadians, lives up to the highest ethical standards, and applies the utmost care and prudence in the handling of public funds.
- Commit to experimentation to improve program delivery.

For Internal Services, the Department will undertake the following initiatives in 2018–19:

- Support innovative approaches to engaging citizens and stakeholders in service design.

- Support innovative approaches in the area of IT procurement.
- Continue to plan and conduct 47 experiments in 23 of its 25 funding programs to help solve existing problems in the delivery of programs.
- Canadian Heritage is leading several experiments and pilots related to Open Government, and will develop a digital strategy in a way that will respond to needs of stakeholders and Canadians.
- Leverage input from Canadians to inform policy development, program and service design and delivery.
- Increase the number and percentage of the Department's open datasets and information available online.
- Use technology to enhance efficient and evidence-based decision-making, such as Artificial Intelligence-enabled decisions and predictive modelling.
- Build on efforts to ensure that Gender-based Analysis Plus and Diversity and Inclusion considerations are integrated in policy and program orientation throughout the Department.
- Continue to foster a healthy and respectful workplace by promoting the importance of mental health, focussing on increasing awareness of the mental health continuum and continuing to implement the 2017–2020 Canadian Heritage Workplace Well-being Action Plan.

Planned results: what we want to achieve this year and beyond
2018–19 Departmental Plan:

- Work on building workforce engagement and enhance management practices through openness, honesty, civility and inclusiveness as well as by experimenting with upward feedback mechanisms such as skip level meetings and internal surveys.
- Broaden our strategic recruitment plan founded on the competencies of the future, with emphasis on diversity.
- Deepen efforts to care for employees with Public Service Pay Centre issues, ensuring punctual resolutions, while ensuring that our human resources and workplace programs are aligned with central agency policies and requirements.

Source: www.canada.ca/content/dam/pch/documents/corporate/publications/plans-reports/departmental-plan-2018-2019/departmental-plan_2018-2019.pdf , 2020

Turning to the scholarly debates on governance and institutions, the established top-down nature of investment in economic development has reinforced economic development as a top-down policy, rather than an exchange relationship between communities and governments. This has emphasised concepts of structure and agency (Peinhert, 2018). Peinhert suggests the exogenous economic and political forces on periods of flux force change upon institutional structures.

The creative sector operates as a parallel mechanism both within and outside the governance and institutional structures. The top-down nature

---

Box 6.3 Investment across the five regions

Breakdown of municipal cultural investment

In each city, the net cultural investment in 2009 was:

- C$27.4 million in Vancouver (population 578,000)
- C$22.4 million in Ottawa (population 812,100)
- C$41.9 million in Calgary (population 988,200)
- C$89.0 million in Montréal (population 1,620,700)
- C$47.5 million in Toronto (population 2,503,300)

These 'net' figures represent the amount invested from the cities' tax bases for that year. In the five cities combined, a net amount of $228.2 million was invested in culture in 2009. Combined, the five cities have a population of 6.5 million. Grants and operating expenditures comprise the largest portions of the overall cultural investment of the five cities:

$82.6 million in operating expenditures (36 per cent of the total)
$89.6 million in grants (39 per cent)
$56.0 million in capital expenditures (25 per cent)

Source: www.creativecity.ca/database/files/library/
Municipal_cultural_investments_5cities.pdf

---

of governance and policy-making around economic development and the creative sector – more specifically tension between the role of central government-focused large-scale renewal initiatives, governance systems and institutional mechanisms and the demands and on-the-ground issues that confront communities – has reinforced the tensions between these two aspects of the creative arts and creative sector more widely.

Box 6.4 The creative sector and exports

Implement the creative export strategy

Global competition is not about looking like everyone else. It's about taking what is unique about our country and telling those stories proudly. Canada's population reflects the world, and this diversity is Canada's competitive advantage.

We are building on our international success by making tailored investments in distribution and promotion. In Budget 2016, we committed a two-year, C$35-million investment fund to support the international discovery and export of Canadian creative works. This also includes support for the participation of Canadian artists and creative industries in cultural events taking place in foreign countries, development of artistic projects, as well as support for outreach events that involve the participation of Canadian creators.

With these funds, we've already begun to see results in four areas.

1   We have rebuilt capacity at home and in key Canadian missions abroad: we hired new cultural and trade officers in key markets including London, Los Angeles, New York, Paris, Berlin, Abu Dhabi, Jakarta, Mexico, Mumbai, South Africa, Shanghai, Tokyo and Washington. These experts are now on the ground, have access to funds to support activities and are ready to give advice to creators on how to access the market, including who potential buyers are, and creating business-to-business opportunities. Two industry advisory groups to the Minister of Canadian Heritage have been struck, one in Shanghai and one in Los Angeles, to help inform our efforts in helping our creative companies to enter or grow their presence in these two markets.

2   We have re-established our presence at international events to promote our creative industries and create new opportunities to make deals and build critical international relationships to access new markets. For example, in August 2017, Canada was the official partner country at Gamescom in Cologne, an event that attracts more than 30,000 trade representatives each year. Canada will also be the Guest of Honour country in 2020 at the Frankfurt Book Fair.

3   We reaffirmed Canada's international leadership in culture and diversity, including at UNESCO, the G7 meeting of the ministers of culture; and through reinvigorating bilateral relationships with key partners such as the United Kingdom, Germany, China and France to open new markets, opportunities and collaborations for our creative industries.

4   We increased investment in key programmes within Canadian Heritage to support international touring, marketing and promotion. New funds have already been allocated to MusicAction and FACTOR through the Canada Music Fund, and to the Canada Book Fund. Support for export activities will be broadened beyond the Canada Book Fund and Canada Music Fund, to help creators and creative entrepreneurs through the Canada Periodical Fund and the Canada Arts Presentation Fund. The focus will be on promoting Canadian creators globally and helping them seize international business opportunities. Telefilm Canada will receive C$2.5 million in 2017–2018 in new funds to position and promote Canadian creators and audiovisual content in key priority markets in Europe and Asia, and to increase support for co-productions.

Today, as part of our Creative Canada vision, we are announcing a new investment of C$125 million over five years to support Canada's first Creative Export Strategy and we will work to enrich this programme as we continue to open up new markets and opportunities for Canada's creative entrepreneurs.

This sustained investment will also ensure the initiatives we have begun will be expanded into the future.

We will support the development of new tools to facilitate access to information on federal exports programmes and market opportunities for Canadian creators, working closely with Export Development Canada, the Business Development Bank of Canada (BDC), the Canadian Trade Commissioner Service (TCS) and our diplomatic missions abroad. The Government will work with partners to strengthen Canada's creative brand and its creators on the international stage.

Creative Canada – policy framework

A new Creative Export Fund will be launched in 2018 to help Canadian creators achieve their international business objectives. We will roll out the details of the new Fund and of our comprehensive Creative Export Strategy in the year ahead.

We will target key markets where there are strong opportunities to promote Canada's creative industries. We will build strong cultural and economic relations with these key countries and present Canada as a destination of choice for investment in the creative industries sector, with a view to opening doors for Canadian companies wishing to export and engage in these markets.

Source: www.canada.ca/content/dam/pch/documents/campaigns/
creative-canada/CCCadreFramework-EN.pdf

Behavioural governance, structure and agency

What is the role of community participation and engagement in this process?

Existing debates around the idea of self-governance are driven by the underpinning idea of ethics and subjectivity that continues to be refracted through varying scales and levels of ongoing existing institutional life (Luxon, 2008; Fraser, 2003; Petersen, 1997). This is also a key divergence from the governance that has enabled the rise of creative arts groups. In the Foucauldian notion of self-governance, the subject is still operated on and through via law-making bodies and established structures. They are self-governing only to the extent that this may be a coping mechanism or reaction against such established structures, but they essentially remain as subjects and objects within the established structured mediating rules of the game. This is markedly different from the roles of creative arts groups. While they, like the notion of self-governance to an extent, have emerged as a reaction to and a product of these establishment structures, they are not subjects or objects in any sense, and this is what makes the understanding of their self-organisation so vital.

These key differences from the Foucauldian notion of self-governance are also a product, evidently, of rapid evolving technological digital platforms to conduct interactions across. The emergence of self-governance as a *response*

Box 6.5 Investment and planning in the creative sector

As part of this investment, the Government invested $550 million to foster the development of the arts in Canada by doubling the budget of the Canada Council for the Arts between 2016 and 2021. These funds will support a new, streamlined and outcomes-based funding model that allows artists, groups and organizations to define their own ambitions and projects with greater flexibility. Through this model, the Council will triple its investment in projects by 2021, a direct investment in innovation and experimentation in the arts. Also by 2021, the Council will triple its investment in Indigenous arts, in part through a new program dedicated to First Nations, Inuit and Métis cultural expression. In addition to the new investment in the Canada Council, the Government invested $675 million in the CBC/Radio-Canada to enable it to become more digital, to support and promote more quality Canadian content to provide more local news and information to Canadians across the country, and to support the next generation of creative talent. We invested in Telefilm Canada and the National Film Board of Canada to boost their work in producing distinctive, relevant and innovative feature film, audiovisual and digital content, and to promote it in Canada and internationally.

These direct new investments in the arts and culture are part of the foundation on which Creative Canada is built and represent an historic investment in our creators and cultural entrepreneurs.

Canada's audiovisual industry is facing significant disruption from changes in consumer habits and business models.

Canadians also find, access and consume content through global online and mobile platforms, in addition to the traditional broadcasting system. With Canadians increasingly watching content online, contributions from the broadcasting sector to the Canada Media Fund have started to decrease in step with their declining revenues.

The Government of Canada is committed to strengthening its support for the creation of high-quality Canadian content at a time when diminishing cable and satellite subscription revenues has meant that the Canada Media Fund has fewer resources available to support independent Canadian productions. As a critical source of funding for our audiovisual creators and producers, we will increase the federal contribution in order to maintain the level of funding in the Canada Media Fund starting in 2018.

This new funding, together with the $134 million we provide to the Fund annually, will help support good jobs, including for our writers, showrunners, producers, directors, actors and crews. To ensure that the Government's investment in the CMF contributes to the Creative Canada vision, we will work with the Canada Media Fund Corporation over the next year to support the further evolution of television and interactive media production in Canada.

We will work with the CMF to examine what more could be done to support development, with a view to build on its history of supporting such high-quality programs as *Unité 9* and *Orphan Black*, and explore what more might be done to enhance early-stage development of content, such as scriptwriting and pitch development. We will also ensure that the CMF Corporation continues to invest at minimum $40 million per year in innovative projects through the Experimental Stream, thus strengthening Canada as a leader in leading-edge interactive digital media content and software applications.

The CMF supports Canadian creative talent in both official languages, as well as Indigenous, official-language minority productions, and diverse language productions. We will look to the CMF to devote more resources to Indigenous productions to ensure that Indigenous creators are supported to tell their own stories and bring them to Canadians and the world. We will also look to the CMF to explore the possibilities to integrate international marketing and promotion earlier in the production process for large-budget projects, thus ensuring that more productions such as *Little Mosque on the Prairie*, *Murdoch Mysteries* and *Mensonges* find audiences not only in Canada but also abroad. Over the longer term, we will look to making further modifications to the program to ensure that the CMF has the tools and the flexibility it needs to adapt its support for the screen-based sector given the rapidly changing environment.

Source: www.canada.ca/content/dam/pch/documents/campaigns/
creative-canada/CCCadreFramework-EN.pdf, 2020

construct to the mediations and operation of institutional life is played out in the areas of discourses of health, esteem and, more latterly, against the canvas of a globalised political economy (Hay, 2006; Fraser, 2003).

Conceptual contribution

However, as we note above, the critical question here is why the individual seeks to actualise a system of self-governance, in this case, through rejecting formal established governance modes and accessing social issues through creative arts groups. This seems to be a step for Foucault in reform, through a radical politics, or a coping mechanism to enable the individual to exist as if outside these institutional constraints, when all the time living within them. The differences here are key. While some as a form of self-governance may see the roles of creative arts groups as merely part of a formal governance process, there are marked differences in both form and purpose. In the first instance, the roles of creative arts organisations are not what we might call established governance: they do not hold legitimacy or need to set regulatory norms, and are not part of an institutional structure. Indeed, the roles of creative arts groups are not to reform or radicalise existing established institutional structures; rather, they are to actually, not *subconsciously*, exist and operate outside of these structures. Although, as Luxon (2008: 384) goes on to argue, Foucault's notion of ethical self-governance comprises: 'relations, their links, their imbrication with those other things, which are wealth, resources, means of subsistence, the territory with its specific qualities'.

Moreover, in achieving and actualising the notion of self-governance, Foucault is highly prescriptive. In achieving self-governance, individuals feel they have become 'no longer dependent on the terms and authority structures of external order' (Luxon, 2008: 391). We assert this is not self-governance in real terms, but instead imagined self-governance. At first glance, it may seem to share some of the aspects Foucault prioritises around the notion: organisation, agency and self-control. In the institutional arena, however, the fundamental and key differences are that, first, the self-organisation of creative arts groups is not at least a formal recognised type of governance; and second, and equally importantly, the established idea of self-governance is that it is an individual reaction to institutional conditions that the individual is reacting against, but within these existing structures and to enable a set of challenges towards achieving a more radical politics. In other words, the goal of self-governance is to reform the institutional arena and the conditions for the individual within those structures.

Legitimacy

The role of the state and the investment in creative arts and the creative economy from central government has several effects in terms of the creative industries and their role in urban economic development. Indeed, the potential risk for funding in these areas to reward existing and established success stories; the difficulties in monitoring the success in increasing policy

---

Box 6.6 Communities and the creative sector

Building communities through arts and heritage

Apply for financial assistance to support a local festival or event commemorating a community anniversary.

Canada Arts Presentation Fund

Apply to the Canada Arts Presentation Fund for financial assistance to organizations that professionally present arts festivals or performing arts series, as well as their support organizations.

Canada Arts Training Fund

Apply to the Canada Arts Training Fund for financial assistance to training institutions that prepare Canadian artists for professional national and international artistic careers.

Canada Cultural Investment Fund

Apply to the Canada Cultural Investment Fund for financial assistance for projects that contribute to the organizational, administrative and financial health of arts and heritage organizations.

Canada Cultural Spaces Fund

Apply to the Canada Cultural Spaces Fund for financial assistance to increase access to cultural spaces for performing arts, visual arts, media arts, and to museum collections and heritage displays.

Canada Council for the Arts

Discover the grants, prizes and services provided by the Canada Council for the Arts to professional Canadian artists and arts organizations.

National Arts Service Organization designation

Apply to be recognized as a national arts service organization by the Government of Canada.

Aboriginal arts

Learn more about Aboriginal arts in Canada and the Aboriginal Art Centre, responsible for the development and preservation of more than 4,000 works of art.

Games of La Francophonie

Cheer on the athletes and artists that take part in these games that are held every four years, bringing together almost 3,000 athletes and artists from 77 member and observer states and governments of La Francophonie.

National Arts Centre

Learn how the National Arts Centre collaborates with artists and arts organizations across Canada to help create a national stage for the performing arts, and acts as a catalyst for performance, creation and learning across the country.

Contributors

- Canada Council for the Arts
- Canadian Heritage
- Indigenous and Northern Affairs Canada

Source: www.canada.ca/en/canadian-heritage/services/
funding/arts-presentation-fund.html

priorities of participation and engagement; and the risk of becoming essentialised from grassroots or bottom-up creative arts or creative industries groups. However, this leads to searching questions of the role of governance and, more particularly, the role of structure and agency in these contexts.

Governmentality

The role of the creative sector in terms of the role of the creative arts in economic development more broadly has been one of social change and bottom-up empowerment. This has been a vehicle for change in urban contexts and in publicising wider social issues in the community. However, the governing contexts for these conditions are necessarily driven by environments of campaigning and seeking change.

Co-production

Aspects of the creative arts have been, as we have seen elsewhere in this book, co-produced with client or community groups. The need for co-produced policy working with communities has tended to be established in contexts where there has been a gap in usual levels of public policy provision and this has been affected to some extent by extreme economic conditions such as austerity, or by other political factors that effect a reduced level of services or a reduced role for existing services. The role of co-production or co-creation mechanisms tend to be used to drive policy innovation, to produce service user-driven policies or to replace established traditional governance services. However, the work with community-facing creative arts groups is distinct from these established ideas. The community have driven creative arts projects and have participated in the development of civic life in the community. These relationships have widened from the creative arts with organisations like Artscape and led to a broader role for the organisation in driving participation in civic life, with the quasi role of governance roles outside of formal institutional behaviours. The bottom-up nature of community creative arts initiatives has been supported by similar approaches to co-production mechanisms, but the impetus of funding and investment in the creative arts and the creative economy centrally has created a firm impetus of institutional focus on participation in and engagement with creative arts. The parallel nature of top-down or bottom-up tensions in the governance of the creative sector has implications for renewal and economic development. Though national-level government policy may highlight investment and the growth of creative economy, the risk of investing in the creative arts in lower affluent economic areas through increased competitive funding may increase participation and ensure the investment in small and medium-sized enterprise (SME) growth for example and heritage is felt by those in all sections of society. This would enable a greater reach in lower socio-economic groups who need to benefit from both short- and long-term economic develop-ment and renewal. For example, investing in existing areas of the strength in the creative economy that have been targeted for growth is surely vital. However, there is also a need to invest in less affluent communities across a range of economic development aspects. This has led to uptake in terms of community engagement and participation, and also in terms of behaviour change in the creative arts.

Filling in a governance gap?

Does this take place in a formal or informal manner?

Bottom-up creative arts groups like Artscape undoubtedly occupy a vital space in terms of engaging communities and maintaining participation in the creative arts. However, there is a broader question around the role of these types of organisations. Why do they focus on a broader remit and are they successful in their missions to address wider social issues in these communities? Through such endeavours, the roles of organisations such as Artscape become broader. As a point of contact addressing social issues in the community – social cohesion, education and skills, and physical renewal of space – these organisations adopt a broader role. In terms of filling in a governance gap, the debate lies in the formal/informal distinction and institutional roles. Though the community is engaged in these projects through the creative arts, this engagement has come through relationships with an organisation that exists and works outside established institutional boundaries. This raises questions around institutional and governance arenas, and how successful they can be in engaging communities and changing behaviour. The roles of top-down investment and policy priorities also engender economic development and renewal though the creative sector: this is just achieved in the opposite way, through national-level investment in growth areas such as digital media.

The role of creative arts organisations like Artscape demonstrates the parallel nature of the creative sector. While this poses challenges to the established ideas of governance, it is overly simplistic to assume that there is a clear distinct gap between the top-down processes of investment and national-level policy and the community-facing creative arts organisations. There is significant overlap in terms of achieving economic development goals, particularly through education. However, the telling factor here is the difference between engaging the community. Though both the national-level policy strategy and the community-facing groups work towards economic development goals, the key differences lie in the success of engaging the community and, of course, time. The problem of achieving sustainable economic development is one that can frustrate the best of policy goals: communities need to see visible signs of progress swiftly; the

Box 6.7 The landscape of creative arts organisations

ONTARIO:

Artscape

Artscape is a not-for-profit, urban development organization that revitalizes buildings, neighbourhoods and cities through the arts. Artscape projects provide affordable space for creativity while generating positive cultural, economic, social and environmental impact.

Art Starts

Art Starts is an arts-based community development organization operating in the City of Toronto. Our mandate is to build healthier communities using the arts. At Art Starts we understand that the arts are a medium for engaging residents, creating a shared sense of identity, identifying challenges and collectively working to overcome them.

Artswell

Our goal is to empower individuals and communities through creativity by exposure to and engagement in the arts. We promote the health of Canadians through the arts by carrying out customized creative, interactive art programs, workshops and projects for the benefit of individuals living with chronic illness or those with special needs, including those who are in hospitals, palliative care, long-term care facilities and community support centres. We offer respite and support to families, staff and caregivers.

Community Arts Ontario

Community Arts Ontario serves as the province's only multidisciplinary, cross-sectional arts network. We provide an effective voice for all individuals, groups and institutions that share our common vision for the arts. Together, we aim to achieve a standard of arts excellence within all regions of Ontario and beyond. As such, we offer unique programs and services to suit a broad range of arts and cultural professionals, community leaders and municipalities.

De-ba-jeh-mu-jig Theatre Group

De-ba-jeh-mu-jig ('Storytellers' in Cree and Ojibway) Theatre Group is a professional community-based non-profit organization dedicated to the vitalization of the Anishnaabeg culture, language and heritage, through education and the sharing of original creative expression with native and non-native people.

Jumblies Theatre

Jumblies promotes art that is woven into life's details, is accessible to all, fosters exploration and excellence, and supports artists of all backgrounds and traditions; and in community that is open-ended and based on people doing something together. Jumblies dismantles boundaries and unites disparate elements. We say, "Everyone is welcome," and grapple with the artistic and social implications of meaning it.

We undertake multi-year residencies, moving through phases of research and development, creation, production and legacy. We discover and transform stories and images; collaborate across disciplines and traditions; bring together people of assorted ages, cultures, abilities and economic levels; employ and mentor established, emerging and newcomer artists; produce new works of art; and create lasting relationships with people and places.

Manifesto Festival: Community Projects

Manifesto is more than just a festival. Everything we do is geared towards fulfilling our mandates and the desires identified through community engagement and feedback, using a multi-disciplinary approach including arts and music workshops, professional development programs, art exhibitions, filmmaking, concerts … whatever's clever.

Sketch

Sketch creates art-making opportunities for young people who are homeless or who are considered to be at risk.

UrbanArts Toronto

UrbanArts initiates arts activities that bring people together in central-west Toronto and city-wide. One of four community arts councils across Toronto, UrbanArts is an incubator for local arts, with a range of programs led by professional artists in visual art, theatre, dance and music.

MANITOBA:

Crossing Communities Art Project

The Crossing Communities Art Project is dedicated to art productions that increase the capacity of women and youth to express themselves through the arts. Crossing Communities is a community-site art project that provides art mentorship to criminalised women and youth through studios and workshops, with the goal of employing visual expression to reduce self-harm, heal from trauma and reduce violence.

NOVA SCOTIA:

4Cs Foundation

The 4Cs Foundation is the leader in community arts in Nova Scotia. Although a grant-giving foundation, 4Cs Foundation has taken a leadership and development role since 2006, providing programming, training and education, as well as ongoing network opportunities. In 2007 the 4Cs Foundation launched its Art Bikers program (see below) – a mobile community arts program that brings free, art-making activities to communities and neighbourhoods across the Halifax Regional Municipality every spring and summer. In 2010 4Cs Foundation hosted the Arts Engage! Symposium and Training – a week-long event with intensive training and weekend workshops on a range of community arts approaches and skill-building opportunities. We brought City Repair from Portland, Oregon to this event, which has resulted in numerous Placemaking and Intersection painting projects in the city. We have offered training in community arts facilitation since 2006 and have trained more than 70 people as community arts facilitators. Also we offer ongoing networking through our Community Arts Circle gatherings which take place every three months.

Art Bikers

Art Bikers is a unique mobile community arts program embracing the talents and gifts of community members and community artists to come together to make art. Our team of community artists ride bicycles pulling colourful trailers full of art materials to neighbourhoods throughout Halifax. Upon arriving, they set up and facilitate collaborative art activities that open up a world of creativity, fun and community connection. Founded in 2007, the Art Bikers have worked with over 4,000 individuals in a wide range of social communities across ages, abilities, languages, race and ethnicities. Open to all community members and delivered in participants' neighbourhoods, Art Bikers fosters creativity between and connections with one another.

SASKATCHEWAN:

The Common Weal Community Arts

Common Weal Community Arts is a provincial arts organization that links professional artists with communities to promote cultural identity and social justice through collaboration and creative expression. Common Weal links artists and communities to animate long-term positive and social change.

We strive to inspire ideas for social change through art. By linking professional artists with communities to engage in collaborative art projects, we empower people – and their communities – to tell their stories in their own voices.

BRITISH COLOMBIA:

Community Arts Council of Vancouver

Creating community with art: Documenting engagement

Currently many Canadian artists are working with communities in exciting and fully engaged ways that situate the artist's practice in both the processes and the products which are created. These are very difficult practices to explain and document, therefore there is a lack of materials that convey the nature of the work.

Video has a particular potential for documenting community-based arts practises as time is an integral element of both forms. The Documenting Engagement Institute supports all artists working in community-based practices by helping both specific sectors (such as grant-makers and educational institutions) and the broader public to become aware of and understand what this work is about and why it is so important.

Redwire Magazine

Redwire is a media and arts organization dedicated to Native youth expression.

Redwire's mandate is to provide Native youth with an uncensored forum for discussion, in order to help youth find their own voice. Redwire is by, for and about Native youth; all content, editorial decisions and associated media projects are initiated and led by youth, inspiring creativity, motivation and action.

Through Our Eyes

Through Our Eyes is a photo documentary program taught and coordinated by a professional photographer, Christine Germano. The objective of this project is to create a legend of a community told through the hearts and eyes of their youth.

Source: www.creativecity.ca/database/files/library/
Municipal_cultural_investments_5cities.pdf

problem of marrying long-term investment with short-term gains; and resistance to change. In terms of achieving economic development goals, there is evidently a pressing need to invest in the creative sector. The broad range of creative activities are evidently vital in driving economic development – through heritage and culture, job creation and growth, education and training, and exports and tourism. Equally, the need to engage communities to ensure successful economic development initiatives is clear. What is compelling about the distinctions between the national-level investment in the creative sector, and the bottom-up role of arts groups is the difference in engaging communities. As noted in Chapter 3, the problems with top-down behavioural public policy and related nudge have failed to change behaviour, in terms of greater participation. However, free entry to museums and galleries has facilitated young people, for example, in engaging with the arts. The success of creative arts groups in engaging communities in the creative arts has evidently demonstrated behaviour change among local communities and the creative arts organisations have successfully used this lens as a mechanism to foster wider civic participation in social life.

Box 6.8 Growth of the sector

Global competition is not about looking like everyone else. It's about taking what is unique about our country and telling those stories proudly. Canada's population reflects the world, and this diversity is Canada's competitive advantage.

We are building on our international success by making tailored investments in distribution and promotion. In Budget 2016, we committed a two-year, $35-million investment fund to support the international discovery and export of Canadian creative works. This also includes support for the participation of Canadian artists and creative industries in cultural events taking place in foreign countries, development of artistic projects, as well as support for outreach events that involve the participation of Canadian creators.

From a static newspaper delivered to the door to mobile access from a bus or café, smartphones and social media have fundamentally changed how Canadians read and share the news. Many Canadians now increasingly find their news or information via platforms like Facebook and Twitter, based on what's been shared by family, friends or groups/organisations that they follow. On social media, news and information is often shared by multiple sources, including professional news organizations, citizen journalists and individuals themselves. This new reality has implications for citizens, journalists and news organizations. For their part, citizens have access to far more news but also must increasingly assess the reliability of news and information they find online. Digital and news literacy skills are critical. Journalists and news organizations, on the other hand, continue to work through the ongoing digital disruption as they seek to meet the expectations of Canadians. Internet companies are critical partners in ensuring citizens' access to news and also to the tools and skills they need to assess the reliability of the news and information found on their platforms. Our clear expectation is that these platforms are partners and must do more to support the creation and distribution of essential news and information. They hold an important responsibility in promoting informed digital citizenship. We will work with internet companies to help jumpstart digital news innovation so Canadian journalists and news organizations are better positioned to succeed in offering Canadians local and regional news in the years ahead. Recognising the dominant role of Facebook and Google in particular in the Canadian news ecosystem, we have begun building partnerships with these platforms to promote digital innovation in news. To this end, this autumn Facebook will launch a partnership with the DMZ at Ryerson University and the Ryerson School of Journalism at FCAD to create a digital news incubator – the first of its kind in Canada – with participants receiving start-up funding from Facebook, mentorship and research support from the Ryerson School of Journalism and a residency at the DMZ. This is North America's leading university-based tech incubator to accelerate innovative ideas that contribute to the digital development of journalism and news organizations. Additionally, they will work with the Canadian Journalism Foundation to promote news literacy in a partnership to be announced later this autumn.

Google will commit to providing new measures to support digital subscriptions and increase discoverability for news publishers, including through the launch of Canada NewsWorks, a program that will develop resources for national, regional and local news publishers. While the programme is still under development, it will focus on convening workshops, roundtables and events, building case studies and best practices, providing a forum to discuss products and platforms, and supporting potential new revenue opportunities for news publishers. We will also continue to work with digital media companies to invest in initiatives that support Canadians of all ages in growing their digital awareness and news literacy skills. We are pleased that the Canadian Journalism Foundation, CIVIX (Student Vote) and Google Canada recently announced a new $500,000 news literacy program that aims to provide over 1.5 million school-aged Canadians with a deeper understanding of the role of journalism in a healthy democracy and how to find and filter information online. As well, Facebook and Media Smarts will soon be launching a two-year partnership on digital news literacy and how to spot misinformation and false news online.

Today, as part of our Creative Canada vision, we are announcing a new investment of $125 million over five years to support Canada's first Creative Export Strategy and we will work to enrich this program as we continue to open up new markets and opportunities for Canada's creative entrepreneurs.

This sustained investment will also ensure the initiatives we have begun will be expanded into the future.

We will support the development of new tools to facilitate access to information on federal exports programs and market opportunities for Canadian creators, working closely with Export Development Canada, the Business Development Bank of Canada (BDC), the Canadian Trade Commissioner Service (TCS) and our diplomatic missions abroad. The Government will work with partners to strengthen Canada's creative brand and its creators on the international stage.

Creative Canada – policy framework

A new Creative Export Fund was launched in 2018 to help Canadian creators achieve their international business objectives. We will roll out the details of the new Fund and of our comprehensive Creative Export Strategy in the year ahead.

We will target key markets where there are strong opportunities to promote Canada's creative industries. We will build strong cultural and economic relations with these key countries and present Canada as a destination of choice for investment in the creative industries sector, with a view to opening doors for Canadian companies wishing to export and engage in these markets.

Create a Creative Industries Council

Headed by the Minister of Canadian Heritage and the Minister of Innovation, Science and Economic Development, we will launch a Creative Industries Council (CIC) to advise the Government on ways to enhance collaboration between industries and amplify the growth of our creative industries.

Bringing together leaders from across creative industries, the Council will focus on concrete objectives to access new markets and coordinate Canada's international presence. The mandate of the Council will include identifying opportunities to develop new partnerships across the sector, ways to leverage an expanded definition of the industries comprising the creative sector to generate jobs and growth, and to assist in developing the Canadian brand to harness global interest and demand for Canadian creative content.

The membership of the Council will be representative of the Canadian creative sector, including both large and small firms as well as gender, regions and official languages, ensuring that diverse perspectives are captured and heard, including from Indigenous communities. Further details regarding the membership of the CIC, as well as its mandate and operations, will be announced over the coming months.

Expand and modernize audiovisual co-production treaties

Audiovisual co-production treaties allow producers to combine their creative and financial resources to develop co-productions that stimulate foreign investment, create jobs, build industry capacity and increase cultural exchange between partner countries. Canada has been a leading co-producer for over 50 years, thanks in large part to treaties with 55 countries.

In the past ten years, Canada has produced over 600 co-productions, with total budgets close to $5 billion. Since 2016, the Government has signed five new treaties with Ireland, China (film), New Zealand, Jordan and Luxembourg, while continuing to advance negotiations with key co-production partners, including France and Australia, toward modernized treaties.

In March 2017, Canada became the first non-European member of Eurimages, the Council of Europe's film co-production fund. This significant step reflects Canada's renewed engagement with Europe more broadly, and opens a new door for the creation and international promotion of Canadian co-productions.

Canada will announce the start of negotiations with other key co-producing partner countries in the months ahead.

Engage internationally on cultural diversity in the digital world

Canada is an active player in international efforts to promote cultural diversity. Canada, in close partnership with France and the Government of Québec, led the development and adoption in 2005 of the *UNESCO Convention on the Protection and Promotion of the Diversity of Cultural Expressions*.

This international treaty has been ratified by more than 140 Member States to date. It recognizes the social and economic character of cultural property and services; reaffirms the right of States to adopt cultural policies; and encourages international cooperation on these issues. Canada's commitment to the UNESCO Convention is a fundamental pillar of our international approach to culture in trade negotiations. It is a reflection of our determination to making diverse voices stand out and be heard by supporting them through effective cultural policies and programs.

In real terms, cultural diversity online stands for the principle that a free and open internet is also a space where diverse perspectives and national content and identities must be respected and presented in a manner that is consistent with universal human rights. It is a recognition that as algorithms and other tools continue to personalize users' online experiences, there remains a fundamental role for governments and digital platforms to ensure that national cultural content is represented in the user experience.

Today, Canada remains more committed than ever to ensuring that the international dialogue on cultural diversity stays relevant in the digital era. We recognize, however, that for countries to meet the objectives of the Convention and properly address the challenges and leverage the opportunities created by digital technologies, they must acknowledge the global, trans-border dimension of these issues. They must also engage a variety of players, including governments, civil society, internet platforms and other private-sector players.

This is why, in addition to our continued work at UNESCO, we are launching a conversation with government organizations, academic leaders, digital platforms and civil society with the goal of building a shared understanding of what challenges and opportunities digital technologies have brought to cultural diversity.

To this end, we will be partnering with the Centre for International Governance Innovation (CIGI) in Waterloo and the Global Digital Policy Incubator (GDPI) at Stanford University, towards an international event in 2018 that would bring together international actors, including governments, digital platforms, civil society and other private actors, to explore practical policy approaches to promote diversity of content and voice in the digital age.

We believe that through multi-stakeholder international engagement, we can promote concrete, collective action on how to support and foster cultural diversity in the digital age, which will in turn contribute to upholding and furthering the objectives of the UNESCO Convention.

Source: www.canada.ca/content/dam/pch/documents/campaigns/
creative-canada/CCCadreFramework-EN.pdf, 2020

Governance theory

Reframing the theory: the role of the creative sector in terms of institutions, governance and behaviour

The following sections of the chapter now move on to revisit the conceptual ramifications for governance theory, following the findings set out above. The Creative City Network has been, as we have seen above, a core focus of national and regional levels of investment in the Canadian creative sector. There are vast policy goals across the creative sector in the Canadian context, which seek to address a range of economic development aspects. These include growth, job creation, skills development and increased tourism. These policy goals have been driven both by the national and regional levels, primarily across cities. The priorities across the creative sector reflect these urban contexts: job creation, growth, digital connectivity and tourism. The creative sector in the Canadian context is a broad range of activities, for example through developing the existing areas of strength such as heritage and crafts. This broad church of creative activities also shows a commitment to fund education, training and exports.

However, we have also seen the vital roles played by bottom-up community-facing groups across Canada, using the creative arts as a means of fostering participation in the creative arts and wider social and civic life. These groups often draw upon the creative arts as a means of addressing a much broader set of issues. For example, the creative arts have acted as a means of participation into a broader set of social issues, such as community cohesion.

These relationships differ from established underpinning modes of informal governance (Ayres, 2017). In order to be lasting and sustainable processes, however, governance design and delivery that will overcome existing challenges to participation and engagement in the creative arts and wider social issues must underpin these. Any aspect of changes in behaviour that results in increased participation must overcome the problems of mistrust in established governance bodies and the validity of evidence on which public policy decisions is based. As noted earlier in this book, these tend to be driven by problems of ideas of perfect or imperfect information, and long-standing mistrust of elites (John, 2017). This is a long-standing issue in engaging and realising changes in behaviours and shifts towards the creative arts and economic development issues among local resident communities. Equally, there is a risk of large-scale economic development initiatives that engender rapid physical or visible change in communities failing to engage these communities. The role of changing behaviour in engaging with the creative arts and through this with wider social issues that are affected by economic development is key to achieving successful and sustainable change, though the complexities of such change are not just confined to physical change. Socially, and more organically, this is also vital in terms of engaging with individuals and communities. The top-down nature of economic development initiatives face challenges of how and when to engage, and of judging the pace of change in changing behaviour. The potential for mistrust in nudges brought about by large-scale economic development initiatives is also significant. This is driven by problems such as rapid change, top-down development and a lack of consultation among communities. The role of creative arts organisations that are community facing and can operate in a de facto 'governance' role, as a point of contact for communities, leads to greater behaviour change such as increased engagement and participation in the creative arts and wider economic development and renewal programmes.

Equally, there can be a tendency in development projects to place too great an emphasis on the complexities of delivery partnerships that can act as a barrier to community engagement. In a federal system, with competencies overlapping or funding driven by both national and regional levels, this may be less of a risk, as responsibilities are clearly delineated. However, complexities of governance such as large partnerships are an enduring problem in enabling engagement from communities. One of the enduring challenges of economic development initiatives is achieving last and enduring outcomes. Sustained community engagement is vital in achieving lasting economic development and renewal outcomes, though both bottom-up and top-down processes. Equally, in developing these practices and behaviours communities' existing networks and partnerships with creative arts groups are key to growing participation in the creative sector and wider social and civic activities in the future.

Box 6.9 Artscape

CREATIVE PLACE-MAKING

2018–2022

The World Cities Culture Forum recently recognized the affordability crisis as the biggest threat to culture in global cities and in 2017 engaged Artscape as an advisor in developing solutions with the potential to address the scale and urgency of the challenge.

One area of related work that Artscape is uniquely qualified to lead involves shifting creative place-making from the margins to the mainstream of urban development. This will be the major focus of Artscape work over the next five years.

Creative place-making leverages the value that artists bring to urban and community development to benefit many parties including the artists themselves. We recognized that a foundational element of mainstreaming creative place-making involves upgrading the package of benefits that accrue to artists engaged in Artscape projects so that they are better equipped to deal with today's realities of digital disruption, precarious work and the affordability crisis. Artscape's new Thriving Artists Initiative is a cornerstone of our new strategic plan. Many of the new programs and services within it will be delivered through the Artscape Daniels Launchpad project that will help thousands of artists realize their potential.

Our efforts to mainstream creative place-making in Toronto will be helped by new policies related to community hubs and inclusionary zoning as well as increased public investment in affordable housing.

Artscape will expand its portfolio from 11 to 18 projects by 2022 with a greater focus on community cultural hubs outside Toronto's core and affordable housing for artist-led families. Under the right circumstances, we will also begin to explore development in the Greater Golden Horseshoe. We will manage this expansion while working hard to ensure that our existing projects remain shining examples of creative place-making where artists and communities thrive.

Artscape's Creative Placemaking Lab will continue to build and share knowledge with more than 100 communities around the world. It will lead the effort in Toronto and globally to help usher in a new era of arts-friendly urban development. We are more committed than ever to our vision of "building a world that engages art culture and creativity as catalysts for community vibrancy, sustainability, prosperity and inclusiveness." Working together with artists and our many partners and stakeholders, we are in a great position to become one of the most powerful new drivers of inclusive growth. We look forward to working with you to build a better world over the next five years.

Source: https://issuu.com/torontoartscape/docs/artscape_vision2017_final, 2019

Governance: targets, collaboration and delivery

The role of top-down investment in the creative sector is necessarily underpinned by targets, such as metrics around job creation, growth, exports, or increases in tourism and the visitor economy. This is a necessity of top-down investment, and undoubtedly aims to foster the economic and social benefits that are common to different varieties of the New Public Management (NPM). As Shand argues:

> We see the role of targets and measurement – in effect, performance management – emphasised both through global level agreements such as Kyoto, Johannesburg and Rio; and in more every day policy settings through commitments to reduce carbon emissions tends to be measured and involve targets … the features of NPM, such as efficiency, outcomes, measurement and targets, remain key elements of policy for combatting climate change, from the individual, societal, national and global levels … that is, the moral, global energy and environmental politics – it is evident that each of these presents vast and complex issues which need to be managed both by nation states (with different and competing priorities) and collectively at the global level. In achieving such compromise, we see performance management involving measurement and targets. Similarly, the NPM focus on efficiency incentivises governments to think about the short term when making policy. This can lead to populist policymaking which favours immediate economic problems or fossil-fuel-driven industries over investment in alternatives such as solar energy, which may be costly in the short term and difficult to sell to voters and the media at times of financial pressure. NPM also has the potential to generate perverse outcomes through measurement of long-term goals. Governments focused on short-term gain and popularity may sign up to long-term

goals that they will never have to be accountable for implementing. This may also institutionalise notions of moral hazard, through measuring aspects of behaviour like recycling rather than changing long-term behaviours.

(Shand, 2018: 231–232)

However, the role of targets is a necessary underpinning mode of measuring the success of top-down investments in the creative sector and the related policy strategies. The success of the creative sector and its role in driving economic development is also dependent on community engagement.

However, the role of creative arts groups in engaging communities so successfully in broader civic and political life through the media of the creative arts suggests the role of networks in governance is one that distances communities from decision-makers. The broad-ranging policy goals at the national level in the Canadian context, set out earlier in this chapter, are driven by the national and regional levels. This governance framework, however, captures a broad range of cultural and heritage activities across the creative sector, as well as aspects such as exports. The multi-level nature of Canadian domestic governance has captured several strands of creative activity and in seeking to develop and invest in these, coalesces the creative sector as a driver for longer-term economic development. What makes the roles of community-facing creative arts groups so vital is their success in not only engaging communities to change behaviour and participate in the creative arts, but, moreover, the means of using the creative arts as a vehicle to participate in wider civic and political affairs and issues. In terms of governance, this is distinct from established views such as the NPG, where partnership of actors in a pluralist state that can drive relations with communities through, for example, the third sector in partnership with local levels of governance. Rather, here we are seeing these ad hoc relationships with communities operating outside the formal partnerships setting. There are, however, caveats to this. Community-facing creative arts groups do, of course, seek funding from national, regional and local governance bodies and related agencies. In this vein, these groups do enter formal arenas and partnerships from time to time, but do not remain within them, and in the main operate outside of these walls.

There is a substantial debate on the definition and limits of the third sector which is beyond the scope of this article (see Kelly 2007). Accordingly, throughout this article we use a fairly broad definition of 'third sector organization' (which also takes in actors known as 'voluntary' or 'non-profit' organizations) to mean any self-governing bodies that are formally organized, independent from the state, non-profit-distributing, and benefit from some sort of voluntarism in their activities. Policy makers have consistently welcomed and supported a role for the third sector in the delivery of public services. There are a number of drivers that might help to explain the increasingly prominent role played by TSOs [third sector organisations]. TSOs are often portrayed as offering unique added value for public services – including the ability to involve people in service delivery, their independence and ability to innovate, their lack of institutional baggage, and their flexibility (Osborne and McLaughlin 2004). For policy makers, the inclusion of TSOs can guarantee more specialist services shaped to the needs of users with complex problems (Smith and Smyth 2010). However, reflecting NPM approaches, UK government policy makers also seem interested in using the third sector to strengthen contestability in public service 'quasi-markets' (Kelly 2007; Painter 2013). We argue that this approach currently co-exists and interacts with an emergent NPG framework, characterized by a broader range of delivery actors, diverse processes of service delivery, and a greater emphasis on co-producing services in collaboration with end users. This has resulted in an increasingly complex state, in which multiple processes and stakeholders form part of intricate and relational public service systems. The successful governance of these public service systems would therefore seem to be both an inevitable consequence of these two forms of plurality and an essential prerequisite for the effective delivery of public services (Radnor and Osborne 2013). It is a significant challenge for TSOs. In practice, the last 15 years have seen significant change in how the third sector interacts with the state in the UK and its devolved nations. The third sector has grown its role in public service delivery. The 1998 'Compact' sought to redefine and formalize the relationship between the state and the third sector (at the UK level, and replicated in Scotland), and a range of capacity-building funding measures introduced in the 2000s (such as the 'Futurebuilders' programme) provided resources to develop the sector's business management and service delivery functions. Both the UK and Scottish governments also produced action plans to support TSOs' roles in the delivery of public services (Cabinet Office 2006; Scottish Government 2008).

(Lindsey *et al.*, 2014: 4)

Concluding remarks

This final case-study chapter has examined the role of the creative sector in Canada. The chapter has focused on this problem in two main ways. First, through looking at the role of national-level funding and policy priorities in core areas of the creative economy. Second, the chapter then moved on to focus on the role of bottom-up creative arts organisations in driving economic development goals such as educational participation and community engagement. In practical policy terms, the Canadian case again demonstrates two sides of the creative sector in economic development.

On the one hand, the importance of national-level targeted investment and policy goals to support this funding, driving economic development outcomes such as increased skills and training, higher employment rates, greater exports from the creative sector and growth across the sector.

On the other hand, there is a burgeoning scene in the creative arts in Canada, driven by bottom-up creative arts organisations that are focused on community arts, engagement and participation. Through working in partnership with communities and other small local actors, events and exhibitions are often key physical features of these projects. However, the economic development and renewal focus of organisations such as Artscape leads not only to greater participation in the creative arts across communities, but also more broadly drives economic development goals through these endeavours, that lead to greater participation in the creative arts, in community and civic life, and greater educative and employment potential.

Conceptually, this chapter has examined the roles of governance, behaviour, and structure and agency. The tensions between the top-down funding and policy directed at core priorities and the bottom-up roles of creative arts organisations both drive the creative sector and economic development more broadly. The different ways in which this takes place, however, lead us to revisit established notions of governance. Working with communities in partnership or co-production has been well established conceptually: what is different in this context is the community drawing on the projects and activities provided by a creative arts organisation as a means of economic development. This is different from the top-down national-level investment in the creative sector, and challenges established ideas of governance, structure and agency, and behaviour.

References

Ayres, S. (2017) Assessing the impact of informal governance on political innovation *Public Management Review* 19 (1): 90–107

Canadian Heritage (2018) *Departmental Plan 2018–19*

Fraser, N. (2003) Rethinking recognition: Overcoming displacement and reification in cultural politics. In Hobson, B. (ed.) *Recognition struggles and social movements: Contested identities, agency and power* Cambridge: Cambridge University Press

Harris, A. and de Bruin, L. (2019) Creative ecologies and education futures. In: Mullen, C. (ed.) *Creativity under duress in education? Resistive theories, practices, and actions* Switzerland: Springer

Hay, C. (2006) Constructivist institutionalism. In: Binder, S., Rhodes, R. and Rockman, B. (eds) *The Oxford handbook of political institutions* Oxford: Oxford University Press

Hill, K. (2012) *Municipal cultural investment in five large Canadian cities: A study prepared for the City of Vancouver, the City of Calgary, the City of Toronto, the City of Ottawa and the Ville de Montréal* Creative City News www.creativecity.ca/database/files/library/Municipal_cultural_investments_5cities.pdf

Hill Strategies (2018) *Canadians' arts, culture, and heritage participation in 2016*

Jaaniste, L. (2009) Placing the creative sector within innovation: The full gamut *Innovation* 11 (2): 215–229

Jacobi, S. (2019) Advancing a progressive trade policy *New Zealand International Review* 44 (1): 13

John, P. (2017) *How far to nudge? Assessing behavioural public policy* Cheltenham: Edward Elgar

Leger, M. (2010) The non-productive role of the artist: The creative industries in Canada *Third Text* 24 (5): 557–570

Lindsay, C., Osborne, S. and Bond, S. (2014) The 'new public governance' and employability services in an era of crisis: Challenges for third sector organisations in Scotland *Public Administration* 92 (1): 192–207

Luxon, N. (2008) Ethics and subjectivity practices of self-governance in the late lectures of Michel Foucault *Political Theory* 36 (3): 377–402

Murray, C. and Gollmitzer, M. (2012) Escaping the precarity trap: A call for creative labour policy *International Journal of Cultural Policy* 18 (4): 419–438

Peinhert, E. (2018) Periodizing, paths and probabilities: Why critical junctures and path dependence produce causal confusion *Review of International Political Economy* 25 (1): 122–143

Petersen, A. (1997) Risk, governance and the new public health. In Petersen, A. and Bunton, R. (eds) *Foucault, health and medicine* Abingdon: Routledge

Shade, L. and Jacobson, J. (2015) Hungry for the job: Gender, unpaid internships, and the creative industries *The Sociological Review* 63 (S1): 188–205

Shand, R. (2018) The role of ethics and targets in environmental governance and the enduring importance of new public management *Political Studies Review* 18 (3): 230–239

Stern, M. and Seifert, S. (2008) *From creative economy to creative society* Philadelphia: The Reinvestment Fund

Stolarick, K., Florida, R. and Musante, L. (2005) *Montreal's capacity for creative connectivity: Outlook & opportunities* Working paper, Catalytix

Suciu, M. and Nasulea, D. (2019) Intellectual capital and creative economy as key drivers for competitiveness towards a smart and sustainable development: Challenges and opportunities for cultural and creative communities. In: Matos, F., Vairinhos, V., Maurício Selig, P. and Edvinsson, L. (eds) *Intellectual capital management as a driver of sustainability* New York: Springer

UNESCO (2014) https://en.unesco.org/countries/canada/events

Volkerling, M. (2001) From cool Britannia to hot nation: 'Creative industries' policies in Europe, Canada and New Zealand *International Journal of Cultural Policy* 7 (3): 437–455

Wyszomirski, M. (2004) *Defining and developing creative sector initiatives* Ohio: Ohio University Press

7 Comparing across the creative sector

Governance, best practice and communities

This chapter now moves on to focus on the key comparisons across the three case-study areas. The chapter will examine the conceptual and theoretical outcomes of the case-study findings. In following on from the three empirical case-study chapters, this chapter will look at the ways in which convergence has occurred across the case-study areas, using the findings from the cases. The initial sections will examine the differences in the respective policy goals of governments across the creative sectors, and will look at which aspects of these models have demonstrated similarities and differences. The chapter will move on to set out each of these models in the cases alongside each other and describe occurrences of governance and behaviour.

Governance theory

The following sections now move on to revisit the theoretical positions covered in each of the case-study chapters. Across each of the case studies, there were distinct similarities in terms of governance design and delivery. However, there were also clear differences in terms of both institutional design and the behaviour of actors in governance of the creative sector. Some of these aspects were driven by underpinning differences in governance and institutional architectures, such as the overlapping nature of competencies in the German context between national and regional levels of governance. Each of the cases has been driven by substantial policy focuses and national-level investments in the creative sector, towards longer-term goals of economic development and renewal. These include job creation; education, skills and training; increased focus on the roles of strands of the creative sector such as heritage, culture and gaming. The roles these aspects play in exports and employment are also targets for growth. Each of the cases, however, also demonstrate a substantial role for bottom-up creative arts groups who are community facing. Why is this important? In terms of the creative sectors outlined across the three cases, these are vast and diverse. Similarly, the goals of economic development initiatives are often also diverse – such as employment, green space, renewed housing, transport infrastructure, education, skills and training.

The co-existence of these two sides of the creative sector, as we have seen in the preceding case-study chapters, seems easy enough. Each of the cases demonstrates contexts where there are both national levels of investment in the creative sectors towards economic development and renewal. However, each of the cases also shows contexts where there are broad ranges of community-facing groups drawing on creative arts to engender economic development and renewal goals. Across the three case studies, we have seen these groups use the creative arts successfully in order to address a range of social issues. Through these projects, the different creative arts organisations have fostered community participation in the creative arts. Through these activities, such projects have addressed a number of economic development and renewal issues, including social cohesion; education; and reframing the use of public spaces to use community-driven murals to replace existing problems with graffiti.

Partnerships and networks

Across each of the three cases, there are roles for partnerships in governance design and delivery. The focus of these tends to be driven by engaging with local actors – schools, charities and local levels of government – and through different projects. These tend, across the cases, not to be the types of large-scale or overly complex designs that can serve as a means of disengagement for communities. They have tended to be driven by funding and project activities rather than the more formal established governance partnership involving multiple levels of delivery and several actors often prevalent in larger economic development initiatives.

Institutions, behaviour and agency

As noted in each of the case-study chapters, these relationships raise pertinent questions for the role of institutions and governance. The official mechanisms of delivery are, as has been set out in the case-study chapters, focusing heavily on the creative sector. The success of bottom-up creative arts organisations in not only engaging communities across the cases, but also in addressing wider economic development issues through this lens has been striking. Set against the longer-term objectives of national governments, this seems a complementary aspect for the creative sector in terms of driving economic development and renewal.

Governmentality

As noted above, however, the need for governments to drive the creative sectors through job creation, skills and training fosters aspects of economic development such as growth. Embedding training in these strategic policy goals also shows a longer-term focus. However, despite the need to invest in areas of strength such as gaming or heritage, there is also a need to foster engagement and participation in communities. To be sure, there are examples of this at both national and local levels across the cases, such as free access for young people to galleries and work with schools in fostering young people and families' participation with galleries. Aspects of the national-level investment, such as the UK focus on the creative sector as part of wider Industrial Strategy, also show the importance of these policy goals for economic development and renewal.

Co-production

Throughout the book, the important nature of participation of communities, and the process of engaging these communities, has been stressed. The issues of top-down nudges and behavioural public policy – examined in Chapter 3 – have failed to engage the public and to change behaviour. In terms of the creative arts, projects may become co-created with communities, though there is also, for some of the creative arts organisations, the related issue of when to let go. In each of the cases, there has been a clear gap (addressed in later sections) for the creative arts to fill, which has led to broader success and engagement in working towards economic development goals.

Informal governance

As noted in the case-study chapters, the notion of informal governance is distinct from what we have seen in the three comparative cases. The underpinning aspects of informal governance (Ayres, 2017) are processes that may shadow and enable processes of the business of governance to take place, which operate away from formalised discussions or policy mechanisms. These informal aspects, however, take place within the established governing arenas and formal institutional spaces. The roles of the creative arts community-facing organisations may resemble informal relationships but are outside the traditional governance arenas and formal policy spaces. Rather, these relationships have been built on enabling the community to engage with the creative arts in a bottom-up manner, as opposed to a top-down arrangement. It is the organic nature of these relationships that have made them so powerful and transformational – and indeed, enduring – that they are able to address community issues and drive economic development through the creative arts in ways that are more problematic for national- or local-level governments.

Legitimacy

Across the three cases of the UK, Germany and Canada, there are clear demonstrable examples of creative arts organisations engaging with communities and fostering participation in the creative arts. Moreover, the institutional and governance mechanisms that have legitimacy through policy-making have not been able to change behaviour towards participation and engagement in the creative arts. More broadly, the lack of formal status of these groups in the eyes of communities seems to have been a large driver for initial engagement in the creative arts. Through their very role as unelected groups outside the traditional governing structures, these groups have been able to establish a kind of legitimacy through trust and participation.

Filling in a governance gap?

With this in mind, the importance of both the national-level investment and the engagement of communities, through creative arts organisations, are vital in driving forward different aspects of economic development. As noted elsewhere in the book, the success of community engagement and participation driven by creative arts organisations such as Refugees' Kitchen address a range of economic development issues. Community cohesion in the German context has been a long-standing issue in terms of housing and immigration. Moreover, the role of engaging communities – both refugees and existing residents – in the creative arts through the kitchen has led to a means of addressing more fundamental and deep-rooted issues that can be barriers to economic development and renewal. The social cohesion that is fostered through the shared participation in the creative arts is driven through the mechanism of the Refugees' Kitchen group, rather than a top-down policy strategy that sets out social cohesion as a goal. Of course, both must work side-by-side, but as noted in the legitimacy discussion above, it is the informal nature of the creative arts organisations that has driven their relationships with the community. These relationships, across the cases, have blossomed into wider social relations between communities and creative arts organisations, occupying the de facto governance role as a point of contact for wider social issues in the community.

Throughout the book, the conceptual argument has focused on the tension between the top-down and bottom-up aspects of the creative sector across the three cases. But why should this be important? To be sure, both top-down and bottom-up aspects of creative sector activity serve to drive urban renewal and economic development. However, what does this mean? Looking across the three cases examined in the book, the bottom-up creative arts organisations that have engaged communities and driven participation to such good effect seem to be filling in something of a governance gap. They have successfully engaged communities through ground-level projects that use the broad range of the creative arts to drive participation in a much broader set of social, political and economic issues. These projects have often fostered social cohesion, educational achievement and a connectivity to place.

This is vital in enabling participation amongst communities and driving urban renewal through the arts. The telling phrase, however, is the governance gap. Across each of the three cases, there are ongoing initiatives that involve large-scale investment in the creative sector. The issue is, if national-level governments are investing in the creative sector to such a large extent – across different cases – then why is this not reaching the types of communities seen across the cases? The aspect of time is clearly important here. Several of the goals of the national strategies are longer term, particularly around job creation and skills development. This makes it difficult to translate industrial and economic development goals into visible successes. Indeed, this is a problem common across economic development initiatives – how to demonstrate progress visibly in a short space of time.

This issue in turn is driven by the issues of mistrust in governments and policy-makers discussed in Chapter 3. The messages of investment in areas that lack jobs or a visible creative sector are more vulnerable to this mistrust, and also to the resistance to perceived attempts at behaviour change, such as increased participation in the creative arts. As examined in the case-study chapters, the governance of the creative sector has produced this tension between top-down and bottom-up aspects of governance, across a mix of actors that straddle the formal and informal aspects of governance.

Conceptually, what does this mean? The three case studies all demonstrate, to varying degrees, multiple levels of decision-making and funding for the creative sector. The cases also show the types of governance at play. Looking at Table 7.1, the cases are drawn from three mature institutional contexts. There is also little variation across the three contexts in terms of the federal/unitary (devolved) difference. The creative sector has been driven by funds from the supranational, national, and regional-local levels, as well as from varying private-sector sources. The supranational funding stream is a clear point of difference: while the UK has received EU funding through structural funds programmes like the European Regional Development Fund (ERDF) and Horizon 2020, the ongoing uncertainty of Brexit has led to planning for replacing or replicating such funding streams. Policy ideas such as the UK Shared Prosperity Fund or the Renewal Fund would take the place of these structural funding mechanisms in the UK to drive economic development, regeneration and regional growth.

The maturity of institutions, as outlined in Table 7.1 above, is important in explaining the apparent gap between top-down and bottom-up aspects of the creative sector. The problem of time, perceived mistrust and failure to change behaviour through top-down mechanisms are both disrupted and complemented by the roles of bottom-up creative arts organisations. Equally, the complexities of governance arrangements in delivering policy (though not confined to the creative sector) are also a factor in creating the space for community-facing organisations to fill a

Table 7.1 Comparative inferences across the cases

Case	Institutional design	Governance delivery	Funding	Types of projects
Germany	Federal	Partnerships; multi-level; networks	EU; national level; regional; local; private sector	Technology; tourism; job creation; education and training
UK	Unitary devolved	Partnerships; multi-level; networks	National government; private-sector investment; EU funds (historically); local level	Digital and technological focus; connectivity; job creation, education and training
Canada	Federal	Partnerships; multi-level; networks	National level; regional level; local level; private-sector investment	Cultural and heritage focus; skills and training; growth of technology; tourism

governance gap. But why should this be important? The answer lies in the ways in which these creative arts organisations have engaged with and sustained community engagement and participation. This has taken place not just in the creative arts arena but rather through using the creative arts as a lens through which to foster participation. This has led to a much wider range of issues that the community is part of. Related to urban renewal and economic development, there are a variety of areas that communities have engaged in across the cases, such as educational development, housing and preventing anti-social behaviour, and social cohesion.

Economic development and urban renewal initiatives have also faced long-standing issues of shifts in physical space, new housing stock and the changing demographic of the community. Each of these aspects represents changes to established community life, and can be difficult to translate into successful renewal. The resistance of communities to changes through economic development initiatives are often driven by the top-down nature of these changes, and the underpinning idea that they are top down; that someone else knows best. The roles of the creative arts organisations across the cases have demonstrated the importance of communities driving these changes and the success of these relationships through bottom-up mechanisms.

Conceptually, the cases have demonstrated the two different aspects of the creative sector. The term sector, moreover, stresses the need to recognise the vital role of creative arts organisations in the large role of the creative arts and creative economy in driving urban renewal and economic development. The two sides of this sector are both key tools in driving forward creativity and development. Theoretically, the types of governance seen across the three cases have much in common. There are clear examples of partnership working across differing levels of governance and through work with SMEs or Universities. These delivery models are successfully driving the investment in creative sector growth and development, and are focused on policy strategies (as set out in the case-study chapters) of job creation, digital growth, growing educational and skills training, and using the creative sense of places to drive tourism and the visitor economy.

The core arguments in this book have stressed the creative sector as, in effect, more than the sum of its parts. As identified across the discussion of established scholarly debates in Chapter 2, and again in each of the case-study chapters, the creative sector is a broad range of activities: these are reflected in the national-level strategies focused on in the case studies, and have a vital underpinning role in driving job creation, economic growth and future education provision and related skills training. To suggest the creative sector, however, is simply the top-down roles of national governments and the need to develop future growth would be to neglect the vital role of bottom-up creative arts organisations who use the creative arts as a means to foster and sustain community engagement in a far wider set of social issues. This participation involves working with galleries, museums and schools. The governance delivery mechanisms, as examined in depth in each of the case-study chapters, are not driven by established formal co-production, but the evidence in each of the case studies demonstrates aspects of this process. Most notably, in each of the cases, there are community actors co-creating and delivering projects.

Conceptually, making sense of governance of the creative sector and its role in economic development means, first, understanding the broad church of the creative industries; and, second, noting the important role played from the bottom-up aspects of the sector. In bringing these two aspects together as a sector, the book argues there is a parallel governance of the creative sector in driving economic development. This parallel governance occurs through the tensions between the top-down and bottom-up roles of creativity. Both of these aspects, top-down funding and policy direction from national-level governments and bottom-up community participation, drive the creative sector and also underpin its role in delivering economic development and urban renewal programmes across the cases.

The need for further comparison

The three cases of the creative sector and economic development examined in the research, drawing upon the comparative case-studies tradition, such as Lijphart's piece 'The Comparable-Cases Strategy' (1975), have sought to demonstrate the breadth of the creative sector both from a top-down and bottom-up perspective. As comparative results, these cases evidently could be used to broaden the comparison of governance of the creative sector and its role in economic development regeneration initiatives in future studies. The following sections examine this point of the importance of the creative sector in driving development.

The role of the creative sector and its role in economic development and renewal can be examined in many diverse countries operating under vastly contrasting systems of governance, public policy goals and institutions. For example, Australia or the USA (at the national or subnational level) can be used as an additional Anglo-Saxon case with the UK, or Australia/USA as a control for the effect on regeneration initiatives of institutional design, as, like Germany and Canada, Australia and the USA are both federal systems. Looking at China would prove a further contrast, evidently primarily in terms of the system of governance, and the node of institutional design. The advantage of the small-*n* or single-case-study research design is again evident in this instance, as the comparative nature of the few cases also allows us to delve into them in some depth. In illuminating the truth of their ontological hunches, some scholars argue that it is desirable and necessary for the researcher to 'get their feet muddy' in the case-study areas on field research. Though large datasets are useful and prove an excellent way of collecting evidence in several diverse samples rapidly, even almost instantly, the historical context and drivers which make up the back story of a case-study area, and its cultural contributing factors, is an essential part of any case-study story.

Inferences and evidence

The federal/unitary question is perhaps the most intriguing when examining inferences and this also provides the widest range of comparable cases. The unitary structure of the UK evidently contributed to a differing model of funding regions and cities than in the German and Canadian cases, where there are regional and national, as well as in the German case, EU-level funding streams. These institutional traits of governance delivery, and the differing roles of actors resulted in the emergence of investments across all the cases. Federal cases where the creative sector is a driver for economic development is taking place present themselves in Australia and in the USA. The inferences outlined above from the findings travel to culturally similar cases, but this creates an issue of testing the assertions robustly. Though small-*n* studies, as outlined earlier in this chapter, allow the comparative scholar to ape the single-case-study narrative, as noted earlier in reference to the Lees (2006) article on the rise of comparative pieces in the study of political science, the issue of culture needs to be treated methodically, so the acid test of the findings is travelling to a culturally dissimilar case, such as China.

The cases examined in this book demonstrate governance and institutional differences set out in comparative research, for example drawing on the Most Different Systems Design method, but (referring to Mill's 1843 method of difference) there is a need to test the inferences from the findings in regeneration programmes in cases which may demand a Most Similar Systems Design method of comparison, or indeed a Paired comparison. These methods and the inferences set out above place the findings from the cases in the creative sectors across the three cases in the broader and changing context of comparative politics, and this is discussed in the sections set out below.

Similarities and differences across the cases

Similarities across the creative sectors examined in this book demonstrate the commonalities across national-level government policies. Across strategies for growth, job creation and broader long-term goals, there is clear investment across the creative sector. Furthermore, the roles of communities have also been key in the creative arts and economic development across the cases. The differing institutional and governance structures across the three cases of the UK, Germany and Canada all demonstrate the important roles of the creative arts in moving economic development and renewal projects forward. Despite the differences in institutional design and traditions in governance, across federal and unitary settings, the community in each case played a vital role. There is a tension between the long-standing social issues of achieving social cohesion, participation and community engagement in the creative arts and in marrying this to the longer-term goals of job creation and growth in the creative sectors across the cases. This chapter has also examined the progress of creative driven projects in the case studies, the targets of these projects and the governance structures that drive them. This leads us to conclude there are clear similarities across the case studies in terms of the role of the creative sector in driving economic development and urban renewal. This takes place in two ways. First, through government driven initiatives and funding; and second, through more bottom-up community-focused creative arts organisations.

These conclusions will be set out in the following chapter, in a discussion of the findings more broadly and, building on the governance and further research sections above, what the findings gathered in the case studies mean for other creative sectors and economic development projects. The final chapter will also revisit the key drivers behind the findings, such as questions of the investment, roles of communities and modes of governance delivery in the cases. Each of the cases showed similarities across both the top-down policy priorities and, equally, the role of community-facing organisations in engaging communities. These two sides of the creative sector both drive aspects of economic development across the cases. Strikingly, each of the three case-study areas shows the creative sector as a broad range of creative and cultural activities; each displays a range of creative arts organisations that have engaged with communities; and policy strategies that aim to invest in the creative sector in the longer term.

Concluding remarks

This chapter has set out the key comparisons across the case studies, examining the core similarities and differences; the conceptual importance of these comparisons; and the potential for further comparative research in the area of the creative sector and economic development. The key governance debates have been set out in detail, drawing on the three case-study chapters and the ways in which governance design and delivery differ or converge. These key conceptual aspects of governance, such as partnerships, co-production and informal governance, need to be revisited as a result of the relations we have seen within the case-study areas between the communities and creative arts groups. There is a clear distinction across the cases between the creative sector as a top-down national-level project and the creative sector as community groups that have engaged with communities and successfully fostered participation in the creative arts. Both of these aspects of the creative sector drive economic development and renewal. The top-down national and regional levels of investment foster job creation, skills and training; lead to growth; and also focus on developing existing strengths such as the gaming industry or the role of the creative sector in tourism. The role of the community-facing groups also addresses aspects of economic development and renewal. These include social and community cohesion, participation in civic life, and educational projects. As noted earlier in this chapter, the governance and institutional approaches have produced similar investments and policy goals in the creative sector despite the differences in design. The role of regions, as one might expect, has been somewhat different in that there is specific competency and delivery in the German and Canadian cases. In the UK case study, there has been a focus in recent national-level policy on funding the regions away from London to a greater extent. The following chapter turns to the conclusions of the research. It is to the issue of further research, contributions to the academic literature by the book and themes of the creative sector and governance in comparative context that the book now turns. Alongside the findings themselves, these key issues will also be reflected upon in the next and final chapter, in the concluding sections of the book.

References

Ayres, S. (2017) Assessing the impact of informal governance on political innovation *Public Management Review* 19 (1): 90–107

Lees, C. (2006) We are all comparativists now: Why and how single-country scholarship must adapt and incorporate the comparative politics approach *Comparative Political Studies* 39 (9): 1084–1108

Lijphart, A. (1975) The comparable-cases strategy in comparative research *Comparative Political Studies* 8 (2): 158–177

8 The creative sector and economic development

Global cases, next steps and reframing theory

Recapping the key findings

This book has examined the role of the creative economy in economic development initiatives across a range of subnational cases. In comparing across these case studies, the book has examined the behavioural governance and institutional designs that underpin these cases. This chapter will begin by examining the key findings across the three empirical cases. It will then go on to summarise the conceptual contribution of the book, focused on the role of structure, agency and behaviour in the governance of the creative economy and underpinning economic development initiatives.

Across the cases, there is a clear focus from national government on investment in existing strength and productivity in the creative sector. These investments are often bound up as part of wider policy agendas, such as the UK Government's Industrial Strategy, or wider creative renewal initiatives such as Canada's focus on investment and growth in areas such as heritage. In each of the case studies, there have been attempts to invigorate participation from communities in the creative sector – through work with galleries, schools and local and regional levels of governance.

There is a disruption, however, across the creative sector. This fracture occurs between the investment from national governments into areas of training and innovation like music, festivals, exports and aspects of digital as targeted growth areas and more bottom-up creative arts organisations. While both the investment through creative sector strategies and more organic bottom-up creative arts organisations seek to use the creative sector as a driver for economic renewal and development, there are barriers to achieving this goal. The distinction between the top-down investment and bottom-up organisations has, as examined in the case-study chapters, both enabled and frustrated aspects of economic renewal and development. For example, the success of Take A Part in the UK case study demonstrates the importance of visibility to communities outside traditional governance institutions and arenas. The trust gained by Take A Part in working with varying projects and communities in Plymouth was, in part, gained by the organisation being seen as trustworthy, and the top-down investment in each of the case studies by national governments seems at odds with notions of mistrust in institutions and public policy-makers.

Learning from across the cases

This book has examined the role of the creative sector in economic development and renewal, and has looked at the governance mechanisms and processes that drive the creative sector. Across the three national cases, there are examples of fostering participation and driving engagement in communities. This has taken place through relationship building and via informal and ad hoc projects. In terms of economic development, these projects have driven solutions to wider and much more complex policy problems common to economic development and renewal initiatives. For example, the focus on social cohesion, education and green issues has led to greater behaviour change and participation, through greater trust and collaboration. Often, these have not been formally codified partnerships or co-creative mechanisms but rather something more fundamental and simple: simply asking communities what they would like to see and do in their respective areas.

The governance and policy-making aimed at driving behaviour change, as noted in Chapter 3, has tended to be top-down and deterministic in nature. Although, as discussed elsewhere in this book, there are prime examples of this in national policy-making, in areas such as health and education, these debates can be extended to the economic development arena also. Across wide-ranging economic development and renewal programmes, there are aspects of policy designed to engender behaviour change. These might be the changing physical nature of an area, with new housing or changing local businesses and shops; green space; or in renewed transport links – such as the work on the Old Oak Common project in the UK. The issues in achieving meaningful economic development across these themes and in engaging communities in the process are driven by a lack of trust in established governing and institutional systems.

Common themes and differences

Each of the creative sector case studies examined in the book demonstrated a number of similarities and differences. There are both practical policy implications and learning for the creative sector across the cases. In terms of similarities, the UK, German and Canadian contexts demonstrated the broad conceptualisation of the creative sector, ranging across diverse areas of industry and activity from the gaming industry to work based in heritage and crafts. The cases each demonstrate tensions between the top-down and bottom-up natures of the creative sectors. In each of the case-study chapters, there are clear directions of travel in terms of economic development and renewal goals. These are targeted through national-level policy strategies that emphasise the need to invest in the creative sector through skills and training. Equally, across the cases there are examples of bottom-up creative arts organisations that are engaged in aspects of development and renewal through working with communities. Conceptually, this is important new knowledge in terms of governance and institutions. The contexts of austerity and disengagement created a larger space for these organisations to work in, but the effect on participation and behaviour change in communities through the creative arts has led to greater trust. Across the cases, there is also evidence that these creative arts organisations are working as de facto governance organisations. This is represented through the creative arts organisations as visible points of contact for their respective communities. However, this is also evident through the wider social and economic development goals the organisations work towards through the medium of the creative arts. These include policy arenas such as asylum, education, community cohesion and economic development. It is the existence of these creative arts organisations outside established traditional governing spaces that gives them this value in achieving trust and engagement with communities. However, what is most intriguing is the ways in which these roles have developed. As trust has increased, the presence of the creative arts organisations has changed into that of governance, driving social change and participation across policy spaces. Moreover, these arts organisations show no signs of transitioning into the main established institutional arenas and becoming formal governance organisations. Though, as set out in the case-study chapters in detail, there is a great deal of existing debate that argues agents will eventually inevitably move into the governance and institutional umbrellas. However, it is the roles of these organisations as agents outside these established formal spaces that has enabled them to drive economic development and renewal in such ways. Again, this is not a post-institutional idea – these are agents operating outwith the institutional and governance arenas, not as a reaction to them. Though there are influences of austerity and migration, the role of the creative arts and participation is the core aim of the groups across the cases, and this has developed into a broader 'governing' role.

Reframing theory and implications for institutions and governance: de facto governance

The findings across the three cases demonstrate that behaviour change among communities has occurred in a bottom-up way. This is in contrast to some of the problems nudge-based policies have encountered. As discussed in Chapter 3, these are issues such as the perceived infringements on individual liberty, the strength of the nudge and the mistrust in information that informs policy. These factors then harm the success of nudge-based public policy. The perceived top-down nature of nudge, the mistrust of the policy and the imperfection of the information given have all been large obstacles in implementing successful nudge-based policy. Indeed, as we saw in Chapters 4–6, the role of creative arts organisations and the creative sector in economic development ruptures some of these established debates within nudge. For example, the nudges in behaviour that saw behaviour change in attitudes to education, widening access to the arts and participation in creative arts such as radio, community participation, education and painting projects across the cases. Drawing on the themes of nudge debates, what do these findings mean for the established notions of behaviourism and nudge? As examined in the sections above, the reframing of structure and agency involves the changing roles and behaviours of creative arts organisations and the creative economy. Set in the context of economic development, creative arts organisations and the creative economy have the ability to nudge behaviours towards themes of change in economic development, such as improved educational attainment, community engagement, greener behaviours and healthier lifestyles. This bottom-up nudge initially shows aspects of the mistrust that have been problematic for policy-makers at national level. The encouragement for change in behaviours, through the creative arts and through economic development, is often problematic in achieving change. However, the roles – as we have seen in the empirical chapters – of creative arts organisations and the wider creative economy saw shifts in the top-down nudge relationship. Nevertheless, as we saw in the case-study chapters, there was still a prevailing problem of mistrust and perceived notions of paternalism. However, as detailed in Chapter 4, there has also been a transition in terms of nudge and trust: the role of the creative arts organisations in being bottom up and, crucially, saying the same things about health, green space and education as a formal governance organisation – but without being a formal governance organisation. This, as we saw particularly in Chapters 4–6, led to the community drawing on the creative arts organisation as a quasi-governance organisation, and therefore allowed these community-facing organisations to influence behaviour through nudge, while remaining outside the institutional arena. This resulted in the community or group engaging in trust with the organisations and in activities such as protests, creative arts exhibitions, local political and social campaigns, graffiti projects, a radio station, and linkages with local schools and more sustainable and community-based usage of green spaces.

Across the cases examined in this book, there is a clear rupture between the top-down nature of government policy in terms of growing the creative sector and the bottom-up nature of creative arts organisations across the cases, that are engaged in community development, growing participation in the creative arts, and often wider social causes that form aspects of economic development and renewal. For example, the role of TAP in working with local schools to engage students and families in the creative arts has not only produced a larger take-up of arts participation. Rather, these relationships have fostered a much broader engagement in civic life, in local politics and, through this, in changing behaviour. The role of organisations such as TAP in the UK case-study chapter, or of the Canadian context in Chapter 6, demonstrate the vitality of organisations that can engage communities due to their existence outside the established governance arenas and institutional structures. Why is this important? In practical terms, the community are able to overcome the kinds of trust issues and feelings of disengagement to public policy that were discussed in Chapter 3.

Governance theory

Reframing the theory: the role of the creative sector in terms of institutions, governance and behaviour

The findings across the three cases show practical policy dimensions for the creative sector, driven by the fissure between top-down and bottom-up aspects of the creative sector. Moreover, the two sides of the sector play clear differing roles in driving economic development and renewal. Conceptually, this is also important in representing challenges to existing ideas of how governance works. The theoretical sections of the chapters, and more broadly across the book, have focused on the disruptions to established modes of working. In particular, the relationships between creative arts organisations and communities have developed from one of community engagement and participation in the creative arts to broader economic development initiatives and governance issues. This is distinct from notions of informal governance, as this is focused on the everyday business that shadows the formalities of governing and policy-making within institutions. Rather, the challenges for established governance thought here are in conceptualising the tension between the top-down and bottom-up aspects of the creative sector.

Challenges also exist in underpinning modes of governance that can be overly complex or difficult to navigate. In order to foster participation in the creative arts and drive the creative sector, these mechanisms need to be visible and have clarity. These delivery processes, in order to overcome existing challenges to participation in the creative sector and demonstrate success in driving the creative arts for economic development, must be accessible to communities. This would combat the problem of mistrust as an obstacle to behaviour change and would foster a greater linkage between the bottom-up creative arts organisations and the top-down policy goals of the creative sector. This would also shift away from long-standing legacy issues in economic development that serve to further create mistrust. This is key to achieving more participatory behaviours and shifts towards the creative sector among resident communities. Large-scale economic development programmes across the cases have set out ambitious and wide-ranging policy agendas that place the creative economy at the heart of development. These are well-funded policy agendas, that address aspects of development such as technological progress, education and training, and bridging the urban-rural divide. The role of behaviour in the creative sector is key to achieving successful and sustainable economic development, though the complexities of such change are not just confined to physical change but in terms of engaging individuals and communities, economic development initiatives face challenges of how and when to engage, and of nudging behaviour too aggressively. The potential for mistrust in nudges brought about by development initiatives is also significant. This is driven by problems such as rapid change, top-down development and a lack of consultation among communities. The role of the creative arts organisations in these de facto 'governance' roles, in modelling and influencing behaviour such as participation in the creative arts, is therefore vital and visible. The role of the creative arts organisations is crucial in achieving trust and participation legacy through more bottom-up engaged practices and in developing these practices and behaviours through both their existing networks and networks which will be grown in the future.

Conceptual contribution

The book reframes established notions of governance and institutions through the lens of the creative arts sector. Through comparing across national case studies, the similarities across the cases show the tension between the two sides of the creative sector. The role of behaviour change in the creative arts across the cases has been driven by the bottom-up organisations, which shows the importance of visibility and relationships developing over time organically. This is in contrast to the top-down impetus from the national government investment in a broad range of the creative industries. To be sure, each of these aspects of the creative sector show an underpinning focus on the governance ruptures and tensions between the top-down direction of investment and the bottom-up driver for participation in the creative arts that fosters economic development initiatives. More broadly, wider wicked issues that are often tackled by renewal initiatives, such as community engagement, education and training, and community cohesion have all been driven by the bottom-up organisations examined in this book.

Limitations of the research

The cases have all focused on the role of the creative economy and creative arts in economic development initiatives, and have been underpinned by the behavioural governance approach. The role of institutional design, however – as examined in Chapter 3 – has also been vital in shaping the policy and funding context for the creative economy and the creative arts across these cases. Further institutional analysis may also reveal path dependence leading to institutional systems that facilitate the growth of the creative economy. The discussion above demonstrates the disruption to the established structure–agency relationship we have seen across the empirical case studies. The following section examines the potential for further research across differing cases, and the practical and conceptual effects these could have in bringing further new knowledge to these established debates around the creative economy and economic development.

This book has focused on the creative sector across three cases, examining its role in economic development initiatives. The comparison has illuminated the focus on a wide range of policy goals in achieving economic development through the creative sector. These examples are a broad church encompassing heritage, digital and exports as areas of investment in the creative sector across the cases. The three case studies, however, all have at their heart mature and well-established institutional frameworks. These are the mechanisms through which investment and nudges take place. Conceptually, the book has focused on the tensions between structure, agency and behaviour, and the underpinning institutional and governance mechanisms, arguing the tension between the top-down and bottom-up actors across the creative sector leads us to revisit assumptions about the roles of structure and agency and the ways in which governance is enacted.

Further research: development and other global cases

To be sure, the research has focused on established creative economies and creative arts organisations across three comparative cases. The cases are all drawn from the West, and are all highly developed post-industrial nations. This brings further questions about the role of the creative arts and the creative economy in development. What would the role of the creative economy look like in a developing nation? Would it accelerate the pace of economic development, or would it be problematic? Further comparable cases would be drawn from the emerging economies; and would necessitate further consideration of the research interrogating the overlap between the visitor, sport, green and night-time economies. The creative economy, for example, has been anchored in the green economy and the sporting economy in the emergence of developing nation states and has been used as a mode of soft power (Grix, 2013). Furthermore, the role of institutional arrangements may be markedly different in developing cases from the examples examined in this book. Institutions that are still undergoing development might mean different effects on behaviours, whether they be less or more regulatory, and if this constrains or enables liberty in behaviours. Furthermore, the importance of maturity of institutions, the success of failure of nudge, and the institutional frameworks are all influences on the success or failure of the creative sector and its role in economic development across the cases. The broad range of activities seen in the case studies as coming under the creative sector umbrella is exacerbated by the overlapping nature of the creative sector. Furthermore, in some cases there is a significant overlap between the green economy and creative economy. The three case-study chapters demonstrated both the distinctions and overlapping tendencies of the creative sector. There is overlap – even allowing for such a broad range of activities included under the tent of the creative sector. This diverse range of creativities includes overlap with the green economy, visitor economy, sports and mega events such as festivals.

Conclusions

This chapter has examined the core findings from the book, and moved on to look at the conceptual contribution of the research. In highlighting the new knowledge, both in terms of moving established debates forward regarding the creative economy and also in terms of the theoretical lenses used to examine debates around behaviourism, structure and agency, the book has moved debates forward. This has been achieved through the examination of behaviours that underpin the governance of creative economy, the creative arts and how these relate to economic development initiatives across comparable cases. The book has drawn new lines through the structure–agency debate through findings across the three cases and the behaviours that underpin the creative economy and its role in economic development. Most prominent among these has been the issue of creative arts organisations assuming governance-type roles in their behaviours; related issues of disrupting structure and agency through this relationship with communities; and the changes in behaviours that are driven by economic development initiatives. Some of these are set in policy spaces such as education, health, the environment, transport and mobility. The creative arts and creative economy also, in this vein, represent change – as noted in the empirical case-study chapters – of the relationship between structure and agency. The behaviours of actors such as creative arts organisations and communities have also shifted towards greater participation in the creative sector. There are also contrasts to the top-down behavioural-driven policy changes of the smoking ban, and the problems of subtleties in nudge-based policy-making, as seen in the five-a-day initiative. The creative arts organisations and creative economy have – in the cases examined in this book, at least – demonstrated what we can term bottom-up nudge. As discussed in the case-study chapters, this reframes structure and agency relationships and roles; shifts behaviours and governance of these behaviours; and also addresses some of the issues of trust and perceived infringements around individual freedom and paternalism that have been so difficult to resolve in the nudge policy-making debates.

The role of the creative sector in economic development and renewal is undoubtedly a driver for positive change. Through initiatives such as investment in the SME sector and employment and training, the creative sector is a driver in delivering economic development and renewal goals. Additionally, through bottom-up creative arts organisations, there is a more informal driver for economic development and renewal through the creative arts.

This has been driven by a lack of trust in established institutional structures, which has led to a lack of success in achieving greater community participation through nudge-based policy or behaviour change. These types of problems have, however, been addressed through several initiatives from, for example, galleries such as the Whitworth Gallery in Manchester in the UK working with local schools in fostering participation. The tension between the top-down and bottom-up roles in the creative sector is difficult to reconcile for policy-makers. These are two sides of the same creative coin. Across each of the cases, in terms of behavioural public policy, structure and agency, the role of behaviour is key to achieving policy goals of participation, community engagement and education and training leading to growth of the sector. Moreover, each of these aspects leads to economic development and renewal through the roles of participation, greater levels of social capital, education, skills, training and employment, as well as investment in communities and regions. From the bottom-up side, there is clear evidence in terms of the structure and agency debate of the problem of institutional walls as a barrier to participation in the creative sector across each of the three national cases.

These two sides of the governance coin in the creative sector demonstrate the tensions between top-down investment in the creative economy and creative arts, and the success of bottom-up community-facing creative arts groups in engendering behaviour change and participation, not just in the creative arts, but in wider political and social issues. In characterising these phenomena, we have seen across the three case studies in this book that there is a clear relationship between the creative arts groups and their respective communities. The top-down investment in the creative sector by national governments in each of our three cases shows a commitment to capturing existing areas of strength in the creative sector and to growing these. Within each of these case studies, the creative sector as a driver for economic development and urban renewal is also clear. The question of time in the success of using the creative sector in this way is key. For example, focuses on longer-term policy goals such as increasing education, training and skills provision for creativity are dependent on the continued health, investment and stimulus of the creative sector. Shorter-term goals such as SME growth will result in an increase in jobs, and will reward areas of strength and innovation. The need for these jobs to grow strong enough to draw in new trainees in the sector is evident, and equally, the political will across each case study to continue to invest in the creative sector in the face of competing sectors, party political change and a shifting and uncertain economic environment.

In practical governance terms, the role of the creative sector across each of the three cases demonstrates top-down investment from national government and a range of governance mechanisms to implement these policy goals. The case-study chapters have examined the role of partnerships and networks, formal and informal notions of governance, and wider philosophical debates around institutions, behaviour and structure and agency. The institutional role of established governance actors in driving economic development through the creative sector emphasises participation and engagement, through aspects such as the take-up of training, and in participation and engagement with the creative sector through a range of pursuits. Examples of these are visiting and experiencing heritage, galleries, museums and crafts. Attempts to drive participation in these areas by governments have met with mixed results. In contrast, however, the stark behaviour change fostered by the community-facing creative arts groups has led to, across each of our three cases, the respective communities showing increased engagement and participation in the creative arts. Moreover, the communities through working with these groups have been able to lead and deliver their own creative arts projects. Perhaps more importantly, they have then used the creative arts as a mechanism to engage with more substantive issues across their local areas.

Conceptually, across the three cases, the role of the creative arts groups leads us to revisit some important theoretical propositions about governance. In examining these theoretical disruptions, the creative arts groups have assumed governance-style roles in supporting their communities and also through their ability to foster engagement with political and civic life. Aspects of the policy agendas from national governments across the cases overlap with these goals: participation across the creative sector, engagement with heritage and culture, visiting galleries, and driving education and training.

In conceptualising this problem, it has led to a governance tension within the broad umbrella of the creative sector across each of our three cases. This tension has emerged between the top-down nature of investment in the creative sector to drive employment, innovation and participation; and the bottom-up role of the creative arts groups. Each side of the creative coin is trying to drive participation and engagement in a range of creative sector activities. Moreover, each side has played a governance role with communities. First, the formal governance actors at the national, regional and local levels; and second, the community arts groups occupying a de facto governance role at street level.

The success of the community-facing creative arts groups in changing behaviour and engaging community actors has assumed a wider remit than the creative arts. Moreover, the tension between the top-down and bottom-up aspects of the creative sector is fortified by the fact the creative arts groups remain outside of established formal governance delivery partnerships, and indeed the broader institutional arenas. As examined in the case-study chapters, established theory argues the agent outside the formal institutions seeks to reframe the rules of the game. After these rules have been modified, the agent then enters the formal institutional arena. In terms of the creative sector, however, we have seen across the three cases an enduring tension between the governance actors within formal mechanisms and those groups outside these walls. Both of these aspects, however, are driving economic development through the means of the creative sector. The co-existence of these two sides of the creative coin, at once governing and not governing, with each in their own way engaging communities and moving the creative sector forward, is striking. These two aspects, however, are not seemingly moving closer together. Rather, they are behaving like parallel lines of governance as they engage and develop the creative sector as a mode of driving economic development.

Reference

Grix, J. (2013) Sport politics and the Olympics *Political Studies Review* 11 (1): 15–25

Index

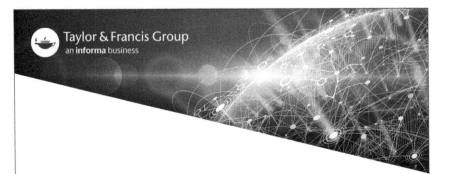

For Product Safety Concerns and Information please contact our EU
representative GPSR@taylorandfrancis.com
Taylor & Francis Verlag GmbH, Kaufingerstraße 24, 80331 München, Germany

www.ingramcontent.com/pod-product-compliance
Ingram Content Group UK Ltd.
Pitfield, Milton Keynes, MK11 3LW, UK
UKHW020949180425
457613UK00019B/601